T·H·E
300-Calorie
One-Dish Meal
C·O·O·K·B·O·O·K

Fast and Fabulous Recipes for
Easy Low-Calorie, Low-Fat Dinners

NANCY S. HUGHES

CONTEMPORARY
BOOKS

CHICAGO

Library of Congress Cataloging-in-Publication Data

Hughes, Nancy S.
    The 300-calorie one-dish meal cookbook : fast and fabulous recipes
for easy low-calorie, low-fat dinners / Nancy S. Hughes.
        p.   cm.
    Includes index.
    ISBN 0-8092-3956-6 (paper)
    1. Low-calorie diet.   2. Low-fat diet.   3. Casserole cookery.
I. Title.   II. Title: Three hundred calorie one-dish meal cookbook.
RM222.H84   1992
641.5′635—dc20   91-42874
                                                          CIP

Copyright © 1992 by Nancy S. Hughes
All rights reserved
Published by Contemporary Books, Inc.
Two Prudential Plaza, Chicago, Illinois 60601-6790
Manufactured in the United States of America
International Standard Book Number: 0-8092-3956-6

This book is lovingly dedicated to my family:

My parents, for teaching me the importance of believing in my dreams and keeping them in focus.

My son Will, for his definite, sometimes well-taken opinions, and for never settling for second-best.

My daughter, Annie, for her elation in the kitchen when I grew weary, and for finding fun in every aspect of cooking.

My son Taft, for being an independent soul and survivor during these writings.

And my husband, Greg, for tasting 8–10 meals a night, every night.

But most of all I dedicate this book to my family for the undying love and support they have given me, from the dreams through the deadlines.

❧ CONTENTS ❧

✦ ACKNOWLEDGMENTS ✦

Special thanks go to Eunice Swift for taking the time to share her mind and expertise with me . . . and to my patient in-laws for the late-night proofreadings.

1
✤ INTRODUCTION ✤

This cookbook contains recipes for more than 140 one-dish meals—all low in fat, all low in sodium, almost all freezable, *and all less than 300 calories per serving.*

From soups and stews, main-course salads, stir-fry, and skillet dishes to oven-roasted entrees and baked casseroles, each meal is prepared in just one pot, one skillet, one broiler pan, or one casserole dish.

The hours before dinnertime can often be the busiest of the day. For parents there are car pools, doctor appointments, and the million and one things that our children require after school. Even for those without children, the end of the day is when energy, patience, and willpower may be ebbing. Needless to say, no one is in the mood to prepare a full meal every night. This book gives some relief by offering satisfying, healthful recipes that are quick and easy to prepare and are consistently low in calories.

There are many advantages to one-dish meals, particularly if they are freezable.

With the following recipes, you'll find a variety of simple freezing methods and tips. They range from completely cooked and frozen entrees to marinated meats that can be thawed and quickly cooked. You might consider making five or six meals ahead to give yourself a week's vacation from cooking!

Everyone seems to be conscious of healthy eating, but trying to keep track of calories, fat, and salt intake can be a lot of trouble. To help, all of these recipes are based on easily obtainable, natural ingredients, are simple to prepare, and are created to please the entire family. All are low in fat, contain less than 500 milligrams of sodium, and are only 300 calories or less per serving.

For the dieter who wants to eat with a clear conscience and enjoy real home-cooked food again . . . the person who does not have time, energy, or desire to face a sink full of dirty pots and pans . . . the person who would like more free time to simply relax, this book can help you enjoy eating again with tasty, nutritious, easily prepared, low-calorie meals.

2
❊ SEAFOOD ❊

Fresh Fish Chowder
Cajun Flounder with Corn and Red Bell Pepper
Belizean Fish
Mediterranean Flounder
Fresh Fish Creole
Blackened Flounder
Flounder Meunière with Lemon Cream Pasta
Red Snapper with Calamata Olives
Swordfish San Pedro
The Gumbo Pot
Twice-Baked Potatoes with Crab and Cheddar Cheese
Crabmeat Alexander
Scallops, Shrimp, and Crab in White Wine Cream
Crab and Shrimp Newburg

Shrimp-and-Crab-Stuffed Eggplant
Seafood New Orleans
Curried Seafood Chowder
Shrimp Creole
Bayou Etouffée
Garlic Shrimp Pesto
Shrimp and Cheddar Pasta
Cheesy Shrimp
Shrimp Pasta with Calamata Olives and Capers
Shrimp and Broccoli Fusilli
The Shrimp Boil
Skewered Shrimp Sesame
Jambalaya
Sweet Dijon Shrimp and Sausage Kabobs

FRESH FISH CHOWDER

Serves 4   **Approximately 8.6 g fat, 421 mg sodium per serving**

A tomato-based chowder packed with onion, potatoes, and corn and seasoned with bacon and hot sauce.

1 slice "lower-salt" bacon
1 cup chopped yellow onion
½ cup chopped celery
¼ cup chopped green bell pepper
2 garlic cloves, minced
1 16-ounce can chopped tomatoes, undrained
1 6-ounce potato, peeled and diced
1 cup fresh or frozen corn kernels
1 5.5-ounce can no-salt-added V8 juice
2 tablespoons cider vinegar
1 tablespoon low-sodium Worcestershire sauce
½ teaspoon black pepper
⅛ teaspoon salt (if desired)
1 medium bay leaf
1 pound fresh catfish or any mild white fish fillets
Hot sauce to taste
2 tablespoons chopped fresh parsley

1. In a dutch oven, preferably cast iron, cook bacon over medium-high heat till crisp. Remove bacon from pot, crumble, and set aside. Drain all but 1 tablespoon bacon grease from pot. To hot bacon grease, add onion, celery, green pepper, and garlic. Sauté 7–8 minutes or until edges begin to brown.

2. Add tomatoes and liquid, potatoes, corn, V8 juice, vinegar, Worcestershire sauce, black pepper, salt, and bay leaf. Bring to a boil and add whole fish fillets, hot sauce, parsley, and crumbled bacon. Reduce heat, cover tightly, and simmer 20 minutes.

3. At end of cooking time, break up any large pieces of fish with a fork. Let chowder stand 10 minutes, remove bay leaf, and serve. Like all stews, this is even better if refrigerated overnight.

MAKE-AHEAD MEAL DIRECTIONS

To Freeze: Complete steps 1–3 of the recipe. Let cool completely. Pour chowder into a 1-gallon freezer bag. Seal bag tightly, allowing no excess air to remain, and freeze. This can be kept frozen for up to 2 weeks.

To Prepare for Serving: Let mixture thaw completely. Pour into a dutch oven or large saucepan and heat thoroughly over moderate heat.

CAJUN FLOUNDER WITH CORN AND RED BELL PEPPER

Serves 4

Approximately 8.6 g fat, 325 mg sodium per serving

1 pound flounder fillets
⅓ cup cornmeal
½ teaspoon Cajun seasoning
Low-calorie cooking spray
1 tablespoon plus 1½ teaspoons butter or margarine
2½ cups frozen corn kernels
½ cup slivered red bell pepper
⅛ teaspoon freshly ground black pepper

1. Rinse fish and shake off excess water. On a plate, combine cornmeal with Cajun seasoning. Coat fish thoroughly with cornmeal mixture.

2. Coat a 10-inch nonstick skillet with cooking spray and heat 1 tablespoon butter over medium-high heat. Add fish and cook 3–4 minutes. Carefully turn fish over and cook 3–4 minutes longer or until fish is opaque in the center. Place fish on a serving platter and set in a warm oven.

3. To drippings, add remaining 1½ teaspoons butter and melt over medium-high heat. When butter is beginning to turn brown, add corn, red pepper, and black pepper. Toss and sauté vegetables 3–4 minutes or until tender. Spoon corn mixture around fish and serve.

MAKE-AHEAD MEAL DIRECTIONS

To Freeze: Complete step 1 of the recipe. (Note: Do not continue to step 2.) Arrange coated raw fish in a single layer on a cookie sheet and freeze overnight.

Gently remove fish from cookie sheet and transfer to a 1-gallon freezer bag. Seal the bag tightly, allowing no excess air to remain, and return to freezer. This can be kept frozen for up to 1 month.

To Prepare for Serving: Let fish thaw completely. Complete steps 2–3 of the recipe.

BELIZEAN FISH

Serves 4

Approximately 6.4 g fat, 477 mg sodium per serving

1 pound fresh flounder fillets
2 tablespoons plus 2 teaspoons low-calorie margarine, softened
2 tablespoons plus 2 teaspoons reduced-calorie mayonnaise
⅜ teaspoon Cajun seasoning
Low-calorie cooking spray
1 tablespoon barbecue sauce
1 teaspoon low-sodium soy sauce
3 cups hot cooked rice (no margarine or salt added during cooking)
2 tablespoons chopped green onion

1. Preheat oven to 350° F.
2. Rinse fillets and lightly shake off excess water. In a mixing bowl, blend margarine, mayonnaise, and Cajun seasoning. Using the back of a spoon, lightly coat both sides of fish fillets with mixture.
3. Coat an 8-inch square baking pan with a low-calorie cooking spray. Arrange fish in center of pan. Dot with barbecue sauce and sprinkle lightly with soy sauce. Cover tightly. Bake for 35–40 minutes, or until fish is opaque in the center.
4. Spoon hot rice around edges of fish. Sprinkle with green onion and serve immediately.

MAKE-AHEAD MEAL DIRECTIONS

To Freeze: Complete step 2 of the recipe. In step 3, use an 8-inch square foil pan and do not bake fish. Do not continue to step 4. With freezer foil, tightly wrap the foil pan containing coated raw fish. Freeze for up to 1 month.

To Prepare for Serving: Let fish thaw completely. Preheat oven to 350° F. Bake fish for 35–40 minutes, or until opaque in the center. Complete step 4 of the recipe.

MEDITERRANEAN FLOUNDER

Serves 4   **Approximately 8.2 g fat, 386 mg sodium per serving**

Fish fillets baked in a tantalizing tomato-caper sauce and served with angel hair pasta.

Low-calorie cooking spray
1 tablespoon extra-virgin olive oil
1 cup thinly sliced yellow onion
3 garlic cloves, minced
½ cup thinly sliced celery
1 cup chopped fresh tomato
2 tablespoons capers, drained
2 tablespoons chopped fresh
   parsley
⅜ teaspoon salt (if desired)
¼ teaspoon black pepper
8 drops hot sauce
2 tablespoons dry white wine
¼ cup water
¼ teaspoon dried oregano leaves
1 pound flounder fillets
3 cups cooked angel hair pasta
   (approximately 6 ounces dry)
1 tablespoon plus 1 teaspoon
   grated Parmesan cheese

1. Preheat oven to 425° F.

2. Coat a 10-inch ovenproof nonstick skillet with a low-calorie cooking spray. Add olive oil and heat over medium-high heat. Add onion, garlic, and celery and cook about 3 minutes. Add tomato, capers, parsley, salt, black pepper, hot sauce, wine, water, and oregano. Bring to a boil, reduce heat, cover tightly, and simmer 5–6 minutes, or until vegetables are tender.

3. Add fish and spoon sauce over it. Bake uncovered for 20–25 minutes, or until fish is opaque in the center. Remove fish to a serving platter. Arrange pasta around fish. Sprinkle pasta with Parmesan cheese and a bit of black pepper, if desired.

MAKE-AHEAD MEAL DIRECTIONS

To Freeze: Complete step 2 of the recipe. (Note: Do not continue to step 3.) Let sauce cool completely. Pour into a 1-pint freezer bag. Seal the bag tightly, allowing no excess air to remain, and freeze. This can be kept frozen for up to 2 weeks.

To Prepare for Serving: Let sauce thaw completely. Shake to mix thoroughly. Preheat oven to 425° F. Arrange fish in an 8-inch square baking dish. Pour sauce over fish and bake uncovered for 20–25 minutes, or until fish is opaque in the center.

Arrange pasta around fish. Sprinkle pasta with Parmesan cheese and a bit of black pepper, if desired.

FRESH FISH CREOLE

Serves 4

Approximately 9 g fat, 322 mg sodium per serving

2 tablespoons plus 2 teaspoons
   butter or margarine
½ cup chopped yellow onion
1 cup chopped celery
¼ cup chopped green bell pepper
1 16-ounce can chopped tomatoes,
   undrained
½ teaspoon low-sodium
   Worcestershire sauce
1 teaspoon reduced-calorie, low-
   sodium catsup
½ teaspoon chili powder
½ teaspoon fresh lemon juice
1 small bay leaf
1 garlic clove, minced
⅛ teaspoon ground red pepper
1 pound flounder fillets
2 cups hot cooked rice (no
   margarine or salt added during
   cooking)
2 tablespoons chopped green
   onion

1. Preheat oven to 350° F.
2. In a large ovenproof skillet, melt butter over medium-high heat until bubbly. Add onion, celery, and green pepper, and sauté 3 minutes. Add tomatoes, Worcestershire sauce, catsup, chili powder, lemon juice, bay leaf, garlic, and red pepper. Reduce heat to simmer and cook 7 minutes longer. Remove bay leaf. Place fish in sauce and spoon sauce over fish. Cover tightly.
3. Bake for 35–40 minutes, or until fish is opaque in the center. Spoon rice around edges of fish and sauce. Sprinkle with green onion and serve.

MAKE-AHEAD MEAL DIRECTIONS

To Freeze: Prepare sauce according to step 2 of the recipe. Let cool completely. Arrange fish in 7″ × 11″ baking pan and pour sauce over fish. Wrap tightly with freezer foil and freeze. This can be kept frozen for up to 1 month.

To Prepare for Serving: Let fish and sauce thaw completely. Preheat oven to 350° F. Complete step 3 of the recipe.

❋ ❋

BLACKENED FLOUNDER

Serves 4   **Approximately 7.3 g fat, 438 mg sodium per serving**

Because this dish creates a lot of smoke during cooking, it's best prepared on an outdoor grill.

1¼ teaspoons cayenne pepper
1 teaspoon lemon pepper
½ teaspoon black pepper
½ teaspoon garlic powder
2 teaspoons dried basil leaves
½ teaspoon dried thyme leaves
¼ teaspoon ground sage
2 tablespoons minced yellow onion
3 tablespoons chopped fresh
  parsley
2 teaspoons fresh lemon juice
½ teaspoon low-sodium
  Worcestershire sauce
1 teaspoon barbecue smoke
  seasoning (I use Liquid Smoke)
1½ pounds fresh flounder fillets
Low-calorie cooking spray
3 tablespoons unsalted butter,
  melted
1 cup sliced yellow onion
1 large red or green bell pepper,
  sliced
⅛ teaspoon salt (if desired)
1½ cups hot cooked rice
Lemon wedges

1. In a 1-gallon freezer bag, combine cayenne, lemon pepper, black pepper, garlic powder, basil, thyme, sage, onion, parsley, lemon juice, Worcestershire sauce, and smoke seasoning. Blend thoroughly and add fish. Seal bag, releasing any excess air. Shake to coat fish thoroughly. Marinate in the refrigerator overnight or at least 2 hours.

2. Heat charcoal in an outdoor grill.

3. Coat a cast-iron skillet with a low-calorie cooking spray. Heat over high heat and add 2 teaspoons of the butter. Heat until butter begins to turn brown, and add onion and red or green pepper. Sauté, stirring, until edges brown. Toss with salt and rice, and place on a serving platter. Cover and set aside in a warm oven.

4. Wipe skillet dry with a paper towel. Coat with a low-calorie cooking spray. Place skillet over high heat for 2–3 minutes. When *extremely hot*, quickly take outside and place over white hot coals in grill (unless you have excellent ventilation—this smokes up a lot!). Add fish and 1 tablespoon of the melted butter, and cook 2–3 minutes until blackened. Turn, add 1 tablespoon plus 1 teaspoon of the melted butter, and cook 2–3 minutes longer.

5. Place fish on platter with vegetables and rice. Serve immediately with fresh lemon wedges.

MAKE-AHEAD MEAL DIRECTIONS

To Freeze: Prepare marinade and coat fish according to step 1 of the recipe. Freeze instead of marinating. (Note: Do not continue to step 2.) This can be kept frozen for up to 1 month.

To Prepare for Serving: Let fish and marinade thaw completely. Shake to blend seasonings. Complete steps 2–5 of the recipe.

FLOUNDER MEUNIERE WITH LEMON CREAM PASTA

Serves 4

Approximately 8.9 g fat, 310 mg sodium per serving

1 pound flounder fillets, cut in 2-inch strips
½ cup plus 3 tablespoons skim milk
½ cup water
2 cups broccoli flowerets
½ cup flour
¼ teaspoon salt (if desired)
Low-calorie cooking spray
1 tablespoon unsalted butter
1 tablespoon vegetable oil
1 teaspoon lemon zest
1 tablespoon dry white wine
⅓ cup evaporated skim milk
⅛ teaspoon garlic powder
1½ cups hot cooked medium egg noodles (3 ounces dry)
1 teaspoon fresh lemon juice
1 tablespoon grated Parmesan cheese
⅛ teaspoon black pepper

1. In a 1-gallon freezer bag, combine the flounder with ½ cup skim milk and let stand for 10 minutes. While fish is soaking, bring water to a boil in a 10-inch nonstick skillet. Add broccoli, cover tightly, reduce heat, and cook 3–4 minutes or until tender but still crisp. Drain well, remove from skillet, and set in a warm oven.

2. Drain fish, discarding liquid. Blot with a paper towel. Sift flour and salt over fish to dust thoroughly. Coat skillet with a low-calorie cooking spray. Over medium-high heat, melt butter with oil. When oil is hot, add fish and cook on one side until it begins to brown, about 3–4 minutes. Turn and cook about 3–4 minutes longer, or until fish is opaque in the center. Place on serving platter and set uncovered in warm oven.

3. Over medium heat, add lemon zest and wine to skillet. Whisk in evaporated milk and garlic powder. Cook, stirring with a whisk, for 1 minute. Add noodles and toss well. Add lemon juice, Parmesan cheese, and black pepper to taste, plus 3 tablespoons skim milk. Arrange broccoli and noodle mixture around fish on serving platter. Serve immediately.

Do Not Freeze

RED SNAPPER WITH CALAMATA OLIVES

Serves 4

Approximately 9.0 g fat, 300 mg sodium per serving

Low-calorie cooking spray
4 4-ounce red snapper fillets
¼ cup finely chopped parsley
1 tablespoon plus 1 teaspoon
    vegetable oil
2 tablespoons red wine vinegar
1 tablespoon chopped capers
½ teaspoon dried basil leaves
¼ teaspoon black pepper
8 calamata olives, pitted and
    chopped fine
¼ teaspoon garlic powder
2 cups hot cooked white rice (no
    margarine or salt added during
    cooking)
3 tablespoons chopped green
    onions

1. Preheat oven to 350° F.
2. Coat a 6″ × 10″ baking dish with low-calorie cooking spray. Arrange fillets in a single layer on the bottom of the pan.
3. In a small bowl, combine parsley, oil, vinegar, capers, basil, pepper, olives, and garlic powder. Blend well and spoon evenly over fillets. Place baking dish in the refrigerator and marinate for 30 minutes.
4. Bake, uncovered, for 20 minutes. Toss hot rice with green onions and transfer to a serving platter. Arrange fish and sauce around rice and serve.

Do Not Freeze

SWORDFISH SAN PEDRO

Serves 4   Approximately 9.3 g fat, 273 mg sodium per serving

Fresh swordfish marinated in cumin and lime, skewered with vegetables and served with a chilled lime-avocado sauce.

¼ cup plus 3 tablespoons fresh
   lime juice
2 teaspoons cumin
¼ teaspoon hot sauce
¼ teaspoon black pepper
1 pound fresh swordfish steaks, cut
   in 1-inch pieces
Low-calorie cooking spray
16 cherry tomatoes
1 medium yellow onion, cut in
   eighths and layers separated
1 yellow bell pepper, cut in 1-inch
   pieces
1 small ripe avocado, peeled and
   seeded
2 tablespoons water
1 teaspoon prepared mustard
¼ teaspoon salt (if desired)
Lime wedges

1. In a small mixing bowl, combine ¼ cup lime juice, cumin, hot sauce, and ⅛ teaspoon black pepper. Mix well. Place swordfish in a 1-gallon freezer bag. Add lime juice mixture. Seal bag, releasing any excess air. Shake well to coat fish thoroughly. Marinate in the refrigerator overnight or at least 2 hours.

2. Preheat the broiler.

3. Coat eight 12-inch skewers and broiler rack with a low-calorie cooking spray. Thread fish and vegetables onto skewers, alternating tomatoes, onion, and yellow pepper. Place on broiler rack and set aside.

4. Place avocado, 3 tablespoons lime juice, water, mustard, salt, and ⅛ teaspoon black pepper in a food processor or blender. Blend well and refrigerate.

5. Broil fish and vegetables 2–3 inches away from heat source for 3 minutes. Turn and broil 2½–3 minutes longer. Spoon ¼ of the chilled sauce on each dinner plate. Add 2 kabobs and fresh lime wedges.

MAKE-AHEAD MEAL DIRECTIONS

To Freeze: Prepare marinade and coat fish as directed in step 1 of the recipe. Freeze instead of marinating. (Note: Do not continue to step 2.) This can be kept frozen for up to 3 weeks.

To Prepare for Serving: Let fish and marinade thaw completely. Shake to blend seasonings. Complete steps 2–5 of the recipe.

THE GUMBO POT

Serves 4

Approximately 5.8 g fat, 496 mg sodium per serving

9 cups water
1 tablespoon liquid crab boil
1 pound flounder fillets
1 slice "lower-salt" bacon
1 tablespoon flour
¾ cup chopped yellow onion
½ cup chopped green bell pepper
1 cup chopped celery
1 16-ounce can no-salt chopped
   tomatoes, undrained
½ pound okra, trimmed and cut in
   ½-inch pieces
½ teaspoon salt (if desired)
⅛ teaspoon black pepper
⅛ teaspoon cayenne pepper
¼ teaspoon garlic powder
⅛ teaspoon dried thyme leaves
1 small bay leaf
1 tablespoon low-sodium
   Worcestershire sauce
⅛ teaspoon hot sauce
1 tablespoon Dijon mustard
2 tablespoons chopped fresh parsley
1 cup peeled and deveined shrimp
   (½ pound)
2 cups hot cooked rice (no
   margarine or salt added during
   cooking)

1. Bring 4 cups water and crab boil to a boil in a dutch oven, preferably cast-iron. Add fish fillets and continue boiling 4–5 minutes, or until fish is opaque. Drain fish, discarding water. Using a fork, flake fish and set aside.
2. Over medium-high heat, cook bacon in dutch oven until crisp. Remove bacon and crumble. Reduce heat to medium and add flour to bacon grease in pot. Blend well and cook 20 minutes, stirring frequently with a flat spatula. Stir in onion, green pepper, and celery, and cook for 5 minutes. Add tomatoes and liquid, and okra. Bring to a simmer and cook for 15 minutes.
3. Add 5 cups water, salt, black pepper, cayenne pepper, garlic powder, thyme, bay leaf, Worcestershire sauce, hot sauce, mustard, parsley, shrimp, and bacon. Bring to a boil, reduce heat, and simmer, uncovered, 1 hour. Add fish and cook 45 minutes longer. Remove and discard bay leaf.
4. Serve over rice.

Note: To enhance flavors, refrigerate overnight, then reheat.

MAKE-AHEAD MEAL DIRECTIONS

To Freeze: Complete steps 1–3 of the recipe. Let gumbo cool completely. Pour into two 1-gallon freezer bags. Seal the bags tightly, allowing no excess air to remain, and freeze. This can be kept frozen for up to 1 month.

To Prepare for Serving: Let gumbo thaw completely. Pour into a dutch oven and heat thoroughly over medium heat. Serve over rice.

TWICE-BAKED POTATOES WITH CRAB AND CHEDDAR CHEESE

Serves 4   Approximately 3.6 g fat, 470 mg sodium per serving

Whipped potatoes in their shells topped with fresh crabmeat and cheddar cheese.

4 8-ounce baking potatoes
1 cup evaporated skim milk
½ cup skim milk
⅜ teaspoon salt (if desired)
¼ teaspoon freshly ground black
   pepper
6 ounces (about 1 cup) crabmeat
2 tablespoons minced yellow onion
½ cup (2 ounces) grated low-
   sodium, reduced-fat cheddar
   cheese
Paprika

1. Preheat oven to 350° F.
2. Wrap each potato individually in aluminum foil. Bake 1 hour.
3. Remove from oven. Split potatoes in half. Gently scoop out insides and place in a mixing bowl, being careful not to tear the outer skin. Add evaporated milk, skim milk, salt, and pepper to potatoes and whip until smooth. Spoon mixture back into potato shells.
4. Top each potato with one-quarter of the crabmeat, onion, and grated cheese. Sprinkle all with paprika. Bake uncovered for 20 minutes.

MAKE-AHEAD MEAL DIRECTIONS

To Freeze: Complete steps 1–3 of the recipe. Top potatoes with crabmeat, onion, cheese, and paprika as directed in step 4. Do not finish baking. Instead, let stuffed potatoes cool completely.

Wrap individually in freezer foil and place in a 1-gallon freezer bag. Seal the bag tightly, allowing no excess air to remain, and freeze. This can be kept frozen for up to 1 month.

To Prepare for Serving: Remove potatoes from freezer bag and let thaw completely. Preheat oven to 350° F. Completely uncover the tops of potatoes and bake for 40 minutes. (Note: When frozen potatoes are thawed, the topping looks watery, but thorough heating perfects their appearance.)

CRABMEAT ALEXANDER

Serves 4

Approximately 8.4 g fat, 500 mg sodium per serving

Low-calorie cooking spray
1 tablespoon unsalted butter
10 green onion tops, sliced
¾ cup skim milk
1 tablespoon flour
1 tablespoon reduced-calorie, low sodium catsup
½ teaspoon lemon juice
⅓ cup dry white wine
1 pound crabmeat
½ teaspoon dried tarragon leaves
⅛ teaspoon black pepper
⅛ teaspoon cayenne pepper (if desired)
15 Ritz brand crackers, crumbled
2 tablespoons grated Parmesan cheese
Freshly ground black pepper

1. Preheat oven to 350° F.

2. Coat a 10-inch ovenproof nonstick skillet with a low-calorie cooking spray. Add butter and melt over high heat. When bubbly, add onions and cook 4 minutes, stirring constantly to prevent burning. Remove onions from skillet and reduce heat to medium. Add milk to skillet and whisk in flour. Cook 4–5 minutes or until thickened, stirring with a flat spatula. Remove from heat. Add catsup, lemon juice, and wine. Gently stir in crabmeat, tarragon, green onions, black pepper, cayenne pepper, and cracker crumbs.

3. Cover and bake for 18–20 minutes, or until heated. Top with Parmesan cheese and freshly ground black pepper. Serve immediately.

MAKE-AHEAD MEAL DIRECTIONS

To Freeze: Complete step 2 of the recipe. (Note: Do not continue to step 3.) Place mixture in an 8-inch square foil pan. Let cool completely, wrap tightly with freezer foil, and freeze. This can be kept frozen for up to 2 weeks.

To Prepare for Serving: Let mixture thaw completely. Preheat oven to 350° F. Place wrapped container in oven and bake for 30–35 minutes, or until thoroughly heated. Top with Parmesan cheese and freshly ground black pepper. Serve immediately.

SCALLOPS, SHRIMP, AND CRAB IN WHITE WINE CREAM

Serves 4

Approximately 8.6 g fat, 462 mg sodium per serving

Low-calorie cooking spray
1 tablespoon butter
¼ cup chopped yellow onion
½ pound scallops
1 cup peeled and deveined shrimp
2 tablespoons fresh lemon juice
⅛ teaspoon freshly ground black
    pepper
½ cup sliced fresh mushrooms
1 cup evaporated skim milk
1 cup skim milk
2 tablespoons flour
2 tablespoons dry white wine
2 tablespoons chopped green
    onion
3 tablespoons chopped fresh
    parsley
6 ounces (about 1 cup) crabmeat
1 cup hot cooked rice (no
    margarine or salt added during
    cooking)

1. Coat a 10-inch nonstick skillet with a low-calorie cooking spray. Add butter. Over medium heat, sauté onions until tender, about 5 minutes. Add scallops, shrimp, 1 tablespoon lemon juice, and black pepper, and simmer 10 minutes. With a slotted spoon, remove seafood and vegetables, and set aside. Add mushrooms to liquid in skillet and simmer, uncovered, 3–4 minutes or until tender. Remove mushrooms with a slotted spoon and set aside with seafood.

2. To liquid, add evaporated milk and skim milk, and whisk in flour. Stir with a flat spatula and cook over low heat, stirring frequently, until sauce is slightly thickened, about 8–10 minutes. Add wine, green onion, 1 tablespoon lemon juice, parsley, and reserved seafood and mushroom mixture. Gently fold in crabmeat.

3. Stir in cooked rice. Serve immediately.

MAKE-AHEAD MEAL DIRECTIONS

To Freeze: Complete steps 1–2 of the recipe. (Note: Do not continue to step 3.) Place mixture in an 8-inch square foil pan. Let cool completely, wrap tightly with freezer foil, and freeze. This can be kept frozen for up to 2 weeks.

To Prepare for Serving: Let mixture thaw completely. Preheat oven to 350° F. Unwrap and bake for 35–40 minutes, or until thoroughly heated, stirring occasionally. Stir in rice and serve immediately.

CRAB AND SHRIMP NEWBURG

Serves 4

Approximately 9.2 g fat, 500 mg sodium per serving

2 tablespoons unsalted butter
1¾ cups skim milk
2 tablespoons flour
Pinch nutmeg
Pinch freshly ground black pepper
3 tablespoons chopped fresh
   parsley
1 2-ounce jar pimientos
4–6 drops hot sauce
1¼ cups peeled and deveined
   shrimp (about 10 ounces),
   cooked
12 ounces crabmeat (about 2
   cups), cooked
2 tablespoons grated Parmesan
   cheese

1. Preheat oven to 350° F.
2. In a 10-inch nonstick skillet, melt butter over medium heat. Stir in milk and whisk in flour. Blend well. Add nutmeg, black pepper, and parsley. Heat, stirring with a flat spatula, about 5–7 minutes until thickened. Remove from heat and gently but thoroughly stir in pimientos, hot sauce, and shrimp. Fold in crabmeat. Pour into individual casserole dishes.
3. Bake for 10–12 minutes, or until heated through. Sprinkle each casserole with 1½ teaspoons Parmesan cheese. Serve immediately.

MAKE-AHEAD MEAL DIRECTIONS

To Freeze: Complete step 2 of the recipe. (Note: Do not continue to step 3.) Place mixture in an 8-inch square foil pan. Let cool completely, wrap tightly with freezer foil, and freeze. This can be kept frozen for up to 3 weeks.

To Prepare for Serving: Let mixture thaw completely. Preheat oven to 350° F. Place wrapped container in oven and bake for 30–35 minutes, or until heated thoroughly. Top with Parmesan cheese and serve immediately.

SHRIMP-AND-CRAB-STUFFED EGGPLANT

Serves 4

Approximately 6.6 g fat, 493 mg sodium per serving

2 small eggplants (about 1 pound each)
1 cup water
Low-calorie cooking spray
1 teaspoon extra-virgin olive oil
1 garlic clove, minced
½ cup finely chopped celery
¼ cup finely chopped yellow onion
¼ cup finely chopped green bell pepper
1 cup peeled and deveined shrimp (about ½ pound)
¼ teaspoon dried basil leaves
¼ teaspoon dried oregano leaves
2 tablespoons chopped fresh parsley
½ teaspoon low-sodium Worcestershire sauce
2 teaspoons Dijon mustard
3–4 drops hot sauce
¼ teaspoon salt (if desired)
2 tablespoons chopped green onion
½ cup (2 ounces) grated Jarlsberg Swiss cheese
½ pound crabmeat
2 slices reduced-calorie bread, toasted and grated

1. Preheat oven to 350° F.
2. Split each eggplant in half lengthwise. Scoop out pulp, being careful not to tear the outer skin, leaving a ¼-inch edge. Chop pulp. Bring water to a boil in a dutch oven. Add chopped eggplant, cover tightly, and simmer 8 minutes or until tender. Drain well and set aside.
3. Coat the dutch oven with a low-calorie cooking spray. Add olive oil and heat over medium-high heat. Add garlic, celery, onion, and green pepper, and sauté 3–4 minutes. Reduce heat to medium and add shrimp, basil, oregano, parsley, and Worcestershire sauce. Cook 5 minutes longer. Remove from heat and stir in mustard and hot sauce. Add eggplant, salt, green onion, and cheese. Stir to blend. Fold in crabmeat.
4. Fill eggplant shells with seafood mixture and top with bread crumbs. Bake for 20 minutes, or until heated thoroughly.

MAKE-AHEAD MEAL DIRECTIONS

To Freeze: Complete steps 2–3 of the recipe. (Note: Do not continue to step 4.) Fill eggplant shells with seafood mixture and let cool completely. Place 2 eggplant halves in each of two 8-inch square foil pans. Wrap tightly with freezer foil and freeze. This can be kept frozen for up to 2 weeks.

To Prepare for Serving: Let eggplant and topping thaw completely. Preheat oven to 350° F. Unwrap eggplant halves and sprinkle with bread crumbs. Bake for 20 minutes, or until heated thoroughly.

❈ ❈

SEAFOOD NEW ORLEANS

Serves 4   Approximately 6.7 g fat, 470 mg sodium per serving

A delicate blend of shrimp, crabmeat, and mushrooms topped with bread crumbs.

Low-calorie cooking spray
4 cups sliced fresh mushrooms
2 tablespoons low-calorie
    margarine
⅔ cup evaporated skim milk
⅔ cup skim milk
1 tablespoon plus 1 teaspoon flour
⅛ teaspoon freshly ground black
    pepper
3 drops hot sauce
1 tablespoon plus 1 teaspoon
    reduced-calorie, low-sodium
    catsup
1¼ teaspoons low-sodium
    Worcestershire sauce
1 teaspoon fresh lemon juice
1 tablespoon plus 1 teaspoon dry
    white wine
3 tablespoons finely chopped
    green onion
1 tablespoon plus 1 teaspoon
    finely chopped red bell pepper
⅓ cup grated low-sodium,
    reduced-fat sharp cheddar
    cheese
1¼ cups peeled and deveined
    shrimp (about 10 ounces),
    cooked
6 ounces crabmeat
1½ slices reduced-calorie bread,
    toasted and grated

1. Preheat oven to 350° F.
2. Coat a 10-inch ovenproof nonstick skillet with a low-calorie cooking spray. Add mushrooms and sauté over medium-high heat for about 5 minutes or until tender. Remove mushrooms and set aside. Wipe the skillet dry with a paper towel.
3. Melt margarine in the skillet. Stir in evaporated milk and skim milk, and whisk in flour. Blend well. Stirring with a flat spatula, cook 4–5 minutes, or until sauce is thickened. Remove from heat, stir in black pepper, hot sauce, catsup, Worcestershire sauce, lemon juice, wine, green onion, red pepper, and cheese. Blend well.
4. Set aside all but ¼ cup sauce, leaving a thin layer on bottom of skillet. Spread a layer of about one-third of the mushrooms on top of the sauce. Spread the shrimp over the mushrooms. Add another one-third of the mushrooms, then spread the crabmeat. Spread the remaining mushrooms over the crabmeat, then pour the remaining sauce over all. Cover with bread crumbs.
5. Bake for 20 minutes, or until heated thoroughly. Heat broiler and brown bread crumbs at least 5 inches away from heat source for 1–2 minutes.

Do Not Freeze

❋ ❋

CURRIED SEAFOOD CHOWDER

Serves 4

Approximately 2.5 g fat, 415 mg sodium per serving

Low-calorie cooking spray
2 cups sliced fresh mushrooms
½ cup chopped onion
1 teaspoon curry powder
2 tablespoons flour
¾ cup evaporated skim milk
1½ cups skim milk
1½ cups water
1 teaspoon low-sodium chicken
   bouillon granules
2 tablespoons sherry
Dash cayenne pepper
⅛ teaspoon nutmeg
⅛ teaspoon ground ginger
¼ teaspoon sugar
1 cup peeled and deveined
   medium shrimp (about ½
   pound)
1 pound scallops
1 tablespoon plus 1 teaspoon fresh
   lemon juice
2 tablespoons finely chopped
   scallion
2 tablespoons finely chopped red
   bell pepper
1 cup frozen green peas

1. Coat a dutch oven, preferably cast-iron, with a low-calorie cooking spray. Sauté mushrooms and onion over medium-high heat for about 4–5 minutes, or until tender. Stir in curry powder and flour, and mix well.

2. Stir in evaporated milk, skim milk, water, bouillon, sherry, cayenne, nutmeg, ginger, and sugar. Bring to a boil. Immediately add shrimp and scallops, and return to a boiling point. Reduce heat and simmer, stirring frequently, 15–17 minutes, or until shrimp begin to curl and scallops turn opaque.

3. Remove from heat. Stir in lemon juice, scallions, red pepper, and frozen green peas. Let stand 10 minutes before serving.

MAKE-AHEAD MEAL DIRECTIONS

To Freeze: Complete steps 1–2, omitting curry powder in step 1. (Note: Do not continue to step 3.) Remove from heat. Stir in lemon juice, scallions, and red pepper, and let cool completely. Add frozen green peas.

Place mixture in a 1-gallon freezer bag. Seal the bag tightly, allowing no excess air to remain, and freeze. This can be kept frozen for up to 2 weeks.

To Prepare for Serving: Let mixture thaw completely. Pour into a large saucepan, add curry powder, and mix well. Cook over moderate heat until thoroughly heated. Do *not* bring to a boil. Let stand 10 minutes before serving.

SHRIMP CREOLE

Serves 4   **Approximately 6 g fat, 468 mg sodium per serving**

Shrimp simmered with bacon, tomatoes, okra, peppers, and onions, seasoned with Creole herbs and spices, and served with fluffy rice.

1 strip "lower-salt" bacon
1 cup chopped yellow onion
3 garlic cloves, minced
6 ounces whole okra, trimmed *or*
   1 10-ounce package frozen okra
½ cup chopped celery
⅛ teaspoon dried thyme leaves
1 cup thin strips green bell pepper
1 16-ounce can chopped tomatoes,
   undrained
Juice of ½ lemon
2 slices fresh lemon with rind
1 teaspoon sugar
1 tablespoon chopped fresh
   parsley
⅛ teaspoon hot sauce
⅛ teaspoon freshly ground black
   pepper
½ teaspoon low-sodium
   Worcestershire sauce
1 small bay leaf
1½ cups peeled and deveined
   shrimp (about ¾ pound)
¼ teaspoon salt (if desired)
2 cups hot cooked white rice (no
   margarine or salt added during
   cooking)

1. In a dutch oven, preferably cast-iron, cook bacon 2–3 minutes over medium-high heat. Remove bacon, crumble, and return to pot with bacon grease. Add onion and cook 2 minutes. Add garlic, okra, celery, thyme, green pepper, tomatoes, lemon juice, lemon slices, sugar, parsley, hot sauce, black pepper, Worcestershire sauce, and bay leaf. Bring to a boil, cover tightly, reduce heat, and simmer 10 minutes.

2. Add shrimp, cover, and cook 20 minutes longer. Remove lemon slices and bay leaf.

3. Stir in salt. Cover and let stand 10 minutes. Serve with rice.

MAKE-AHEAD MEAL DIRECTIONS

To Freeze: Complete steps 1–2 of the recipe. (Note: Do not continue to step 3.) Place mixture in an 8-inch square foil pan. Let cool completely, wrap tightly with freezer foil, and freeze. This can be kept frozen for up to 1 month.

To Prepare for Serving: Let mixture thaw completely. Preheat oven to 350° F. Place wrapped pan in oven and bake for 45 minutes, or until thoroughly heated. Stir in salt and serve over hot rice.

BAYOU ETOUFFEE

Serves 4   **Approximately 6.8 g fat, 475 mg sodium per serving**

Shrimp and vegetables cooked with Cajun seasonings and rice.

Low-calorie cooking spray
1 cup chopped yellow onion
3 scallions, chopped
½ green bell pepper, chopped
½ red bell pepper, chopped
½ cup chopped celery
1 garlic clove, minced
1 tablespoon plus 2 teaspoons
   unsalted butter or margarine
1 tablespoon plus 2 teaspoons
   flour
2 cups peeled and deveined
   shrimp (about 1 pound)
1½ cups water
2 tablespoons fresh lemon juice
1 small bay leaf
⅛–¼ teaspoon hot sauce, to taste
3 tablespoons chopped fresh
   parsley
⅛ teaspoon cayenne pepper
⅛ teaspoon freshly ground black
   pepper
½ teaspoon salt (if desired)
2½ cups hot cooked rice (no
   margarine or salt added during
   cooking)

1. Coat a 10-inch nonstick skillet with a low-calorie cooking spray. Heat 1 minute over high heat. Add onion, scallions, green and red peppers, celery, and garlic. Sauté 5–6 minutes, or until edges turn a rich brown. Remove vegetables and set aside.

2. Add butter and flour to skillet and cook over medium-low heat, stirring constantly, until the mixture becomes a rich brown, about 2–3 minutes. Add cooked vegetables, shrimp, water, 1 tablespoon lemon juice, bay leaf, hot sauce, parsley, cayenne pepper, black pepper, and ¼ teaspoon salt. Stir well and increase heat to boil. Reduce heat and simmer uncovered for 20 minutes. Remove bay leaf. Stir in remaining 1 tablespoon lemon juice and ¼ teaspoon salt.

3. Cover and let stand 10 minutes. To enhance flavor, refrigerate overnight, then reheat. At time of serving, spoon over rice.

Note: If a thick consistency is desired, combine 2 tablespoons cornstarch with 2 tablespoons cold water. Add to pot at end of step 3 and cook 2–3 minutes longer, until thickened.

Variation: Substitute 1 whole green bell pepper for the ½ green and ½ red pepper.

MAKE-AHEAD MEAL DIRECTIONS

To Freeze: Complete steps 1–2 of the recipe. (Note: Do not continue to step 3.) Let mixture cool completely and place into a 1-gallon freezer bag. Seal bag tightly, allowing no excess air to remain, and freeze. This can be kept frozen for up to 1 month.

To Prepare for Serving: Let mixture thaw completely. Place in a medium saucepan and heat thoroughly over medium heat. At time of serving, spoon over hot rice.

GARLIC SHRIMP PESTO

Serves 4

Approximately 6.1 g fat, 498 mg sodium per serving

¾ cup firmly packed fresh spinach
  leaves
¼ cup grated Parmesan cheese
1 teaspoon dried basil leaves
¼ teaspoon salt (if desired)
1 tablespoon sesame seeds, toasted
4 garlic cloves, minced
½ cup plain nonfat yogurt
Low-calorie cooking spray
1 teaspoon extra-virgin olive oil
1¾ cups peeled and deveined
  medium shrimp (approximately
  14 ounces)
¼ teaspoon ground red pepper
¼ teaspoon freshly ground black
  pepper
1 tablespoon minced yellow onion
2 tablespoons water
2 tablespoons fresh lemon juice
3 cups hot cooked spaghetti (no
  salt add during cooking)
½ teaspoon lemon pepper
1 fresh lemon, cut in wedges

1. Place spinach, 3 tablespoons Parmesan, basil, ¼ teaspoon salt, sesame seeds, half of the garlic, and yogurt in a blender or food processor. Blend thoroughly and set aside.

2. Coat a 10-inch nonstick skillet with a low-calorie cooking spray. Add oil and heat 1 minute over medium-high heat. Add remaining half of the garlic and sauté 1 minute. Add shrimp, red pepper, black pepper, and onion. Sauté until shrimp are opaque and curling, about 5-6 minutes. Add water and lemon juice, and stir well. Toss with spinach mixture.

3. Toss shrimp and pesto with hot spaghetti. Top with lemon pepper and 1 tablespoon Parmesan cheese. Serve with lemon wedges.

MAKE-AHEAD MEAL DIRECTIONS

To Freeze: Complete steps 1–2 of the recipe. (Note: Do not continue to step 3.) Let cool completely. Place mixture in a 1-quart freezer bag. Seal the bag tightly, allowing no excess air to remain, and freeze. This can be kept frozen for up to 2 weeks.

To Prepare for Serving: Let shrimp mixture thaw completely. Place in a medium saucepan over medium heat. Cook uncovered, but do not boil, for about 5 minutes, or until heated. Complete step 3 of the recipe.

❧ ❧

SHRIMP AND CHEDDAR PASTA

Serves 4

Approximately 8.5 g fat, 469 mg sodium per serving

Low-calorie cooking spray
2 teaspoons butter or margarine
½ cup finely chopped yellow onion
½ cup finely chopped green bell
 pepper
1½ cups sliced fresh mushrooms
⅓ cup tomato sauce
2 cups cooked spaghetti
½ cup drained and finely chopped
 unsalted canned tomatoes
 (about 5 ounces)
¾ cup grated low-sodium,
 reduced-fat cheddar cheese
⅛ teaspoon salt (if desired)
⅛ teaspoon freshly ground black
 pepper
1¼ cups peeled and deveined
 shrimp, cooked (cooked with
 crab boil seasoning, if possible)
 (approximately 10 ounces)
⅓ cup light sour cream

1. Preheat oven to 375° F.
2. Coat a 10-inch ovenproof nonstick skillet with a low-calorie cooking spray. Add butter and melt over medium-high heat. When bubbly, add onion and green pepper. Cook 3 minutes. Add mushrooms and cook 2 minutes more. Add tomato sauce, spaghetti, tomatoes, cheese, salt, black pepper, and shrimp.
3. Stir in sour cream. Bake uncovered for 25–30 minutes, or until heated thoroughly.

MAKE-AHEAD MEAL DIRECTIONS

To Freeze: Complete step 2 of the recipe. (Note: Do not continue to step 3.) Place shrimp mixture in an 8-inch square foil pan. Let cool completely, wrap tightly with freezer foil, and freeze. This can be kept frozen for up to 1 month.

To Prepare for Serving: Let mixture thaw completely. Preheat oven to 350° F. Stir in sour cream and bake uncovered for 40 minutes, stirring occasionally.

CHEESY SHRIMP

Serves 4

Approximately 8.9 g fat, 495 mg sodium per serving

5 slices reduced-calorie bread, toasted, crust removed, and cubed
1½ cups peeled and deveined shrimp, cooked (about ¾ pound)
1 cup (about ¼ pound) grated low-sodium, reduced-fat cheddar cheese
⅓ cup grated yellow onion
½ teaspoon low-sodium Worcestershire sauce
2 dashes hot sauce
¼ teaspoon dry mustard
2 egg whites
2 tablespoons low-calorie margarine, melted
½ cup skim milk
⅛ teaspoon salt (if desired)
⅛ teaspoon freshly ground black pepper
2 large tomatoes, halved
4 teaspoons fresh lime juice
¼ teaspoon dried oregano leaves
3 tablespoons chopped fresh parsley

1. Preheat oven to 350° F.
2. Spread cubed toast in bottom of an 8-inch square pan. In a mixing bowl, combine shrimp, cheese, onion, Worcestershire sauce, hot sauce, dry mustard, egg whites, margarine, and skim milk. Spoon over toast. Sprinkle with salt and pepper.
3. Place tomato halves on a foil-lined oven rack. Spoon 1 teaspoon lime juice over each tomato half. Sprinkle with oregano.
4. Bake tomatoes and uncovered shrimp casserole for 20 minutes. Remove casserole from oven and let stand 5 minutes. Remove tomatoes from oven. Top all with fresh parsley and serve immediately.

MAKE-AHEAD MEAL DIRECTIONS

To Freeze: Complete step 2 of the recipe, using an 8-inch square foil pan. (Note: Do not continue to step 3.) Let cool completely, wrap tightly with freezer foil, and freeze. This can be kept frozen for up to 2 weeks.

To Prepare for Serving: Let mixture thaw completely. Preheat oven to 325° F. Prepare tomatoes as directed in step 3. Unwrap foil container and bake uncovered with tomatoes for 25–30 minutes.

Remove casserole from oven and let stand 5 minutes. Remove tomatoes from oven. Top all with fresh parsley and serve immediately.

SHRIMP PASTA WITH CALAMATA OLIVES AND CAPERS

Serves 4

Approximately 9.9 g fat, 347 mg sodium per serving

Low-calorie cooking spray
1½ cups peeled and deveined
   shrimp (about ¾ pound)
1 teaspoon olive oil
4 garlic cloves, minced
¾ cup chopped yellow onion
1 16-ounce can chopped tomatoes,
   drained
1 cup sliced fresh mushrooms
5 calamata olives, pitted and
   sliced thin
1 teaspoon capers, chopped and
   drained
1 tablespoon red wine vinegar
1 small bay leaf
2 teaspoons dried oregano leaves
1 teaspoon dried basil leaves
¼ teaspoon black pepper
¼–½ teaspoon red pepper flakes
¼ cup low-sodium chicken broth
¼ cup dry white wine
¼ cup chopped fresh parsley
2 cups hot cooked spaghetti (no
   salt added during cooking)

1. Coat a dutch oven, preferably cast-iron, with a low-calorie cooking spray. Add shrimp and cook over high heat 2 minutes, stirring constantly. Remove shrimp from pot. Set aside. Wipe dutch oven dry with paper towel.

2. Recoat the same dutch oven with low-calorie cooking spray. Add the olive oil and heat over medium-high heat. Add garlic and onion and cook over medium-high heat for 2–3 minutes. Add tomatoes, mushrooms, olives, capers, vinegar, bay leaf, oregano, basil, black pepper, red pepper flakes, broth, wine, and shrimp. Bring to a boil, stirring well. Reduce heat, cover tightly, and simmer 30 minutes. Remove bay leaf and let stand 10–15 minutes.

3. Stir in parsley. Place hot spaghetti on serving platter and spoon shrimp mixture over it.

MAKE-AHEAD MEAL DIRECTIONS

To Freeze: Complete steps 1–2 of the recipe, omitting capers. (Note: Do not continue to step 3.) Let shrimp mixture cool completely. Place in a 1-gallon freezer bag. Seal the bag tightly, allowing no excess air to remain, and freeze. This can be kept frozen for up to 2 weeks.

To Prepare for Serving: Let mixture thaw completely. Shake to blend well. Pour into a medium saucepan and add capers. Heat thoroughly over medium heat. Stir in parsley. Spoon over hot spaghetti.

SHRIMP AND BROCCOLI FUSILLI

Serves 4

Approximately 3.3 g fat, 420 mg sodium per serving

¾ cup water
1½ cups broccoli flowerets
1 cup peeled and deveined
  shrimp, cooked (about ½ pound)
1½ cups skim milk
1 tablespoon cornstarch
½ teaspoon chicken bouillon
  granules
⅛ teaspoon black pepper
¼ cup plus 2 tablespoons grated
  Parmesan cheese
4 cups hot cooked fusilli or any
  corkscrew pasta (no salt added
  during cooking)

1. Bring water to a boil in a dutch oven. Add broccoli, reduce heat, cover tightly, and simmer 3 minutes or until broccoli is tender but still crisp.

2. Place shrimp in a colander. Pour broccoli and liquid over shrimp to heat shrimp and drain broccoli at the same time.

3. In a small mixing bowl, combine skim milk, cornstarch, chicken bouillon granules, and black pepper. Mix well and pour into dutch oven. Bring to a boil over medium-high heat and stir with a flat spatula until thickened, about 1–2 minutes. Remove from heat, stir in ¼ cup Parmesan cheese, and mix well. If sauce is too thick, thin with 1–2 tablespoons skim milk.

4. Toss fusilli with sauce. Add shrimp and broccoli, tossing until thoroughly coated. Sprinkle with remaining 2 tablespoons Parmesan cheese and serve immediately.

Do Not Freeze

THE SHRIMP BOIL

Serves 4   **Approximately 4.7 g fat, 490 mg sodium per serving**

Fresh shrimp, corn, and potatoes boiled together with spices and served with a seafood cocktail sauce.

2 quarts plus 1 tablespoon water
1 crab boil seasoning bag or 2 tablespoons crab boil liquid
8 small new potatoes (about 1 ounce each)
2 medium ears of corn, halved crosswise
1½ pounds unpeeled medium headless shrimp
½ cup reduced-calorie, low-sodium catsup
2 tablespoons fresh lemon juice
2 tablespoons prepared horseradish
½ teaspoon low-sodium Worcestershire sauce
⅛ teaspoon hot sauce
⅛ teaspoon freshly ground black pepper
1 tablespoon plus 1 teaspoon low-calorie margarine, melted

1. Combine 2 quarts water and crab boil in a dutch oven. Bring to a boil, add potatoes, and boil 7 minutes. Add corn to potatoes in pot and boil 7 minutes. Add shrimp, return to boil, reduce heat, and simmer 12–15 minutes, until shrimp are opaque. Remove pot from heat and let shrimp and vegetables stand in hot water 10 minutes.

2. In a small mixing bowl, combine catsup, lemon juice, 1 tablespoon water, horseradish, Worcestershire sauce, hot sauce, and black pepper. Set aside.

3. Drain shrimp and vegetables. Serve with seafood cocktail sauce, using about 3 tablespoons sauce per serving of shrimp and 1 teaspoon margarine per serving of vegetables.

Do Not Freeze

SKEWERED SHRIMP SESAME

Serves 4   **Approximately 7.9 g fat, 490 mg sodium per serving**

Shrimp marinated in honey, soy sauce, and ginger, skewered with bacon, pineapple, and peppers, and sprinkled with toasted sesame seeds.

1 tablespoon plus 2 teaspoons low-sodium soy sauce
¼ cup sherry
2 tablespoons honey
½ teaspoon freshly grated ginger root
⅛ teaspoon hot sauce
2½ cups peeled and deveined shrimp (about 1¼ pounds)
Low-calorie cooking spray
4 slices "lower-salt" bacon, each cut into 8 pieces
1½ cups fresh pineapple tidbits
1½ green bell peppers, cut into 1-inch pieces
1 medium yellow onion, cut into eighths and layers separated
3 tablespoons sesame seeds, toasted under broiler

1. Preheat broiler.
2. In a 1-quart freezer bag, combine soy sauce, sherry, honey, ginger root, and hot sauce. Blend well and add shrimp. Seal bag, releasing any excess air. Shake to coat shrimp thoroughly. Marinate for 1–2 hours in refrigerator.
3. Coat eight 12-inch skewers with a low-calorie cooking spray. Remove shrimp from freezer bag, reserving marinade. Thread shrimp onto skewers, alternating with bacon, pineapple, green peppers, and onions (one shrimp next to each of the other items). Place skewers on a broiler rack coated with low-calorie cooking spray.
4. Broil 2–3 inches from heat source for 3 minutes. Turn, baste with reserved marinade, and broil 3 minutes longer, or until shrimp are opaque and begin to curl. Sprinkle with toasted sesame seeds and serve immediately.

Do Not Freeze

SWEET DIJON SHRIMP AND SAUSAGE KABOBS

Serves 4

2 7-ounce baking potatoes
¼ cup dark brown sugar, packed
¼ cup Dijon mustard
⅜ teaspoon hot sauce
¼ teaspoon curry powder
1¼ cups peeled and deveined
    medium shrimp with tails on
    (about 10 ounces)
6 ounces turkey kielbasa links,
    halved lengthwise and cut into
    1-inch pieces
Low-calorie cooking spray
1 medium yellow onion, cut into
    eighths and layers separated
1 green bell pepper, cut into 1-
    inch pieces
2 teaspoons low-calorie margarine
Freshly ground black pepper

Approximately 7.2 g fat, 471 mg sodium per serving

1. Preheat oven to 350° F.
2. Wrap potatoes individually in aluminum foil. Bake for 1 hour.
3. While potatoes are baking, combine sugar, mustard, hot sauce, and curry in a mixing bowl. Mix well. Stir in peeled shrimp and sausage and coat thoroughly.
4. Coat eight 12-inch skewers with a low-calorie cooking spray. Thread skewers alternately with shrimp, sausage, onion, and green pepper. Place on a broiler rack coated with low-calorie cooking spray and broil 2–3 inches away from heat source for 3 minutes. Turn, and broil 2½–3 minutes longer, or until shrimp are opaque and begin to curl. Place 2 skewers on each plate to serve.
5. Split potatoes and serve each half with margarine and freshly ground black pepper.

Do Not Freeze

JAMBALAYA

Serves 4   **Approximately 6.4 g fat, 496 mg sodium per serving**

Slices of sausage, chicken, and shrimp simmered with tomatoes and other vegetables and richly seasoned with herbs and spices.

Low-calorie cooking spray
6 ounces turkey kielbasa, cut into ⅛-inch slices
6 ounces boneless chicken breast meat, cut into 1-inch pieces
1¼ cups peeled and deveined shrimp (about 10 ounces)
1 cup chopped celery
1 cup green bell pepper strips
1 cup chopped yellow onion
4 garlic cloves, minced
1 16-ounce can no-salt tomatoes undrained
1 10-ounce can low-sodium chicken broth
2 tablespoons chopped fresh parsley
½ teaspoon low-sodium Worcestershire sauce
1 small bay leaf
½ teaspoon dried oregano leaves
¼ teaspoon dried basil leaves
¼ teaspoon ground red pepper
1 tablespoon dark brown sugar, packed
2 tablespoons Dijon mustard
⅓ cup uncooked white rice
⅛ teaspoon freshly ground black pepper
1½ teaspoons cornstarch
1 tablespoon water

1. Coat a dutch oven, preferably cast-iron, with a low-calorie cooking spray. Add sausage and brown over medium-high heat, stirring frequently, 4–5 minutes. Stir in chicken and shrimp. Cook 3 minutes longer, or until shrimp has just turned pink and opaque. With a slotted spoon, remove all and set aside.

2. To any remaining pan drippings, add celery, green pepper, onion, and garlic. Sauté 4 minutes, stirring frequently. Stir in tomatoes and liquid, chicken broth, parsley, Worcestershire sauce, bay leaf, oregano, basil, red pepper, brown sugar, mustard, rice, and black pepper. Bring to a boil. Add chicken and shrimp and any accumulated liquid. Reduce heat, cover tightly, and simmer 20 minutes. Remove bay leaf.

3. In a small glass, combine cornstarch and water. Blend well and stir into pot. Cover and cook 2 minutes longer. Remove pot from heat and let stand 10 minutes. To enhance flavor, refrigerate overnight, then reheat.

MAKE-AHEAD MEAL DIRECTIONS

To Freeze: Complete steps 1–3 of the recipe, except do not refrigerate at the end of step 3. Place mixture in an 8-inch square foil pan. Let cool completely, wrap tightly with freezer foil, and freeze. This can be kept frozen for up to 1 month.

To Prepare for Serving: Let mixture thaw completely. Preheat oven to 350° F. Place wrapped container in oven and bake for 50–55 minutes, stirring midway.

3
❖ CHICKEN ❖

Chicken and Dumpling Noodles
Pineapple Chicken à l'Orange
Chicken Almondine
Chicken Madeline
The Blue-Plate Special
Chicken with New Potatoes and Vegetables
Curry-Rubbed Chicken with Acorn Squash
Lemon Chicken Fusilli
Chicken Tetrazzini
Chicken Brie
Home-Style Chicken and Rice
Lemon Chicken with Artichokes
The Bagged Bird
Jalapeño-Lime Chicken
Country Chicken Pot Pies
Chicken and Stuffing Casserole
Oriental Baked Chicken
Chicken Enchiladas

Peppered Chicken and Onions
Rosemary Chicken with Rice
Chicken with Herbed Country Mustard on Hot French Bread
Eunice's Chili Chicken Stew
Saturday Night Tacos
Barbecued-Chicken Tortillas
Smoked Black Bean, Red Pepper, and Chicken Stew
Chicken Mozzarella
Tarragon Buttered Chicken
Herbed Breaded Chicken
The All-American Basket
Sicilian Chicken with Pasta
Barbecued Chicken–Stuffed Potatoes
Sweet Cradles of India
Hot and Spicy Sesame Chicken
Honey-Glazed Oriental Chicken and Spinach Salad
Chinese Chicken Stir-Fry
Citrus-Walnut Chicken with Currants

CHICKEN AND DUMPLING NOODLES

Serves 4

Approximately 3.4 g fat, 498 mg sodium per serving

6 cups plus 2 tablespoons water
3 5½-ounce skinless chicken breast
  halves, all fat removed
1 celery stalk, cut into fourths
1 tablespoon minced yellow onion
½ teaspoon chicken bouillon
  granules
6 ounces uncooked dumpling
  noodles
1 tablespoon chopped fresh
  parsley
2 tablespoons cornstarch
¼ teaspoon butter substitute (I use
  Molly McButter)
½ teaspoon salt (if desired)
¼ teaspoon freshly ground black
  pepper

1. In a 2-quart saucepan, bring 6 cups water to a boil. Add chicken, celery, and onion. Return to boil. Reduce heat, cover tightly, and simmer 30 minutes. Remove chicken and set aside.

2. Increase heat to high, and add chicken bouillon granules and noodles to broth. Bring to boil, reduce heat, and simmer uncovered about 20–22 minutes, or until noodles are tender. While noodles are cooking, debone chicken. Add chicken and parsley to cooked noodles.

3. In a small mixing bowl, combine 2 tablespoons cold water with cornstarch and butter substitute. Add to pot with salt and black pepper, and cook 5 minutes longer, or until slightly thickened. Remove celery, if desired, and serve.

MAKE-AHEAD MEAL DIRECTIONS

To Freeze: Complete steps 1–3 of the recipe. Place mixture in an 8-inch square foil pan. Let cool completely, wrap tightly with freezer foil, and freeze. This can be kept frozen for up to 1 month.

To Prepare for Serving: Let mixture thaw completely. Preheat oven to 350° F. Unwrap mixture and toss gently with a fork to separate noodles. Bake for 45–50 minutes, or until thoroughly heated.

PINEAPPLE CHICKEN A L'ORANGE

Serves 4

Approximately 6 g fat, 138 mg sodium per serving

½ cup water
3 cups julienned carrots
Low-calorie cooking spray
4 6-ounce skinless chicken breast
　halves, all fat removed
¼ cup pineapple preserves
2 teaspoons horseradish
½ teaspoon orange zest
2 teaspoons butter, browned

1. Preheat oven to 350° F.
2. In a 10-inch ovenproof nonstick skillet, bring water to a boil and add carrots. Reduce heat, cover tightly, and simmer 3 minutes. Drain carrots, remove from skillet, and set aside.
3. Coat skillet with a low-calorie cooking spray and heat 1 minute over high heat. Add chicken, meat side down, and brown without turning for 2 minutes. Remove pan from heat and turn chicken so meat side is up. In a small bowl, combine preserves with horseradish and orange zest. Spoon over chicken. Arrange carrots around chicken.
4. Bake uncovered for 30–35 minutes. At time of serving, drizzle browned butter over carrots.

MAKE-AHEAD MEAL DIRECTIONS

To Freeze: Complete steps 2–3 of the recipe. (Note: Do not continue to step 4.) Place mixture in an 8-inch square foil pan. Let cool completely, wrap tightly with freezer foil, and freeze. This can be kept frozen for up to 1 month.

To Prepare for Serving: Let mixture thaw completely. Preheat oven to 350° F. Place wrapped container in oven and bake for 45–50 minutes, or until chicken is no longer pink in the center. Drizzle carrots with browned butter and serve.

CHICKEN ALMONDINE

Serves 4

Approximately 4.7 g fat, 474 mg sodium per serving

Tender chicken in cream sauce, tossed with noodles and almonds.

Low-calorie cooking spray
10 ounces chicken breast meat, cut
 into ½-inch pieces
1 garlic clove, minced
¼ teaspoon freshly ground black
 pepper
1½ cups skim milk
1 teaspoon chicken bouillon
 granules
2 tablespoons flour
⅛ teaspoon salt (if desired)
1 tablespoon finely chopped fresh
 parsley
3 cups hot cooked egg noodles
 (about 6 ounces dry) (no
 margarine or salt added during
 cooking)
2 tablespoons plus 1 teaspoon
 sliced almonds, toasted under
 broiler

1. Coat a 10-inch nonstick skillet with a low-calorie cooking spray and place over medium heat. Add chicken, garlic, and black pepper, and sauté until cooked, about 3–4 minutes. Remove chicken from skillet.

2. Add milk and chicken bouillon granules to pan drippings. Stir well, scraping sides and bottom with a flat spatula. Whisk in flour and blend well. Add chicken, salt, and parsley. Cook until slightly thickened, stirring with a flat spatula, about 3–4 minutes.

3. Toss with hot noodles and top with almonds.

MAKE-AHEAD MEAL DIRECTIONS

To Freeze: Complete steps 1–2 of the recipe. (Note: Do not continue to step 3.) Let chicken and sauce cool completely. Place mixture in a 1-quart freezer bag. Seal the bag tightly, allowing no excess air to remain, and freeze. This can be kept frozen for up to 1 month.

To Prepare for Serving: Let mixture thaw completely. Pour into a medium saucepan and heat thoroughly over medium heat. Toss with hot noodles and top with almonds.

CHICKEN MADELINE

Serves 4   **Approximately 8.9 g fat, 490 mg sodium per serving**

Breaded baked chicken with hot spinach-and-cheese-stuffed tomatoes.

1 teaspoon flour
¼ cup evaporated skim milk
1 10-ounce package frozen
  chopped spinach, thawed and
  squeezed dry
3 ounces jalapeño cheese, cut into
  ¼-inch cubes
2 tablespoons finely chopped
  yellow onion
¼ teaspoon garlic powder
½ teaspoon low-sodium
  Worcestershire sauce
⅛ teaspoon black pepper
4 medium tomatoes
Low-calorie cooking spray
4 5½-ounce skinless chicken breast
  halves, all fat removed
⅜ teaspoon lemon pepper
½ teaspoon dried oregano leaves
2 tablespoons chopped fresh
  parsley
1 tablespoon grated Parmesan
  cheese
½ slice reduced-calorie bread,
  toasted and grated

1. Preheat oven to 400° F.
2. In a mixing bowl, combine flour and milk, and whisk until well blended. Add spinach, cheese cubes, onion, garlic powder, Worcestershire sauce, and black pepper. Mix thoroughly.
3. Slice tops off tomatoes and scoop out pulp. Fill tomato cups with spinach mixture. Place on a broiler rack coated with a low-calorie cooking spray. Bake 12 minutes.
4. Place chicken on rack with stuffed tomatoes. In a small bowl, combine lemon pepper, oregano, parsley, Parmesan cheese, and bread crumbs. Mix well and sprinkle evenly over chicken. Return chicken and tomatoes to oven and bake 22–25 minutes, or until chicken is done. Arrange on a platter and serve immediately.

MAKE-AHEAD MEAL DIRECTIONS

To Freeze: Complete step 2 of the recipe. (Note: Do not continue to step 3.) Place spinach mixture in a 1-quart freezer bag. Seal the bag tightly, allowing no excess air to remain, and freeze. This can be kept frozen for up to 1 month.

To Prepare for Serving: Let spinach mixture thaw completely. Shake bag to mix well. Preheat oven to 400° F. Complete steps 3–4 of the recipe.

THE BLUE-PLATE SPECIAL

Serves 4   Approximately 6.3 g fat, 483 mg sodium per serving

A wholesome dish of chicken, rice, and turkey sausage.

Low-calorie cooking spray
2½ ounces hot Italian turkey
   sausage
¾ pound chicken breast meat, cut
   into 1-inch pieces
1 cup chopped yellow onion
½ cup chopped red bell pepper
½ cup chopped celery
½ cup uncooked white rice
½ cup well-drained and slivered
   canned water chestnuts
¼ cup chopped fresh parsley
¼ teaspoon ground sage
⅛ teaspoon freshly ground black
   pepper
⅔ cup condensed cream of chicken
   soup, undiluted
⅓ cup buttermilk
1 tablespoon fresh lemon juice
⅛ teaspoon garlic powder
Paprika

1. Preheat oven to 350° F.

2. Coat a 10-inch ovenproof nonstick skillet with a low-calorie cooking spray. Over high heat, brown sausage for about 2 minutes. Drain and discard excess grease. Place sausage on paper towels to remove additional grease. Wipe skillet dry with a paper towel.

3. Recoat the same skillet with low-calorie cooking spray and brown chicken over high heat, stirring constantly, for 1 minute. With a slotted spoon, remove chicken from skillet. Reduce heat to medium-high. To any pan drippings, add onion, red pepper, and celery. Sauté about 3 minutes, or until richly browned and tender but still crisp. Add rice, water chestnuts, 2 tablespoons parsley, sage, black pepper, soup, buttermilk, lemon juice, garlic powder, sausage, and chicken. Sprinkle with paprika and top with remaining 2 tablespoons parsley.

4. Bake covered for 50–60 minutes, or until rice is done.

MAKE-AHEAD MEAL DIRECTIONS

To Freeze: Complete steps 2–3 of the recipe, omitting the paprika and parsley topping. (Note: Do not continue to step 4.) Place mixture in an 8-inch square foil pan. Sprinkle with paprika and top with remaining 2 tablespoons parsley. Let cool completely, wrap tightly with freezer foil, and freeze. This can be kept frozen for up to 1 month.

To Prepare for Serving: Let mixture thaw completely. Preheat oven to 350° F. Place wrapped container in oven and bake for 60–70 minutes, or until rice is cooked.

CHICKEN WITH NEW POTATOES AND VEGETABLES

Serves 4

Approximately 3.8 g fat, 458 mg sodium per serving

¼ cup flour
Low-calorie cooking spray
4 5½-ounce skinless chicken breast halves, all fat removed
½ cup chopped celery
1 cup sliced yellow onion
1 garlic clove, minced
¼ teaspoon freshly ground black pepper
¼ teaspoon dried thyme leaves
¾ teaspoon chicken bouillon granules
3¼ cups water
12 small new potatoes (about 1 ounce each), halved
¼ teaspoon salt (if desired)

1. In a dry dutch oven, preferably cast-iron, stir flour over medium heat until it turns from white to off-white in color, about 7–8 minutes. Remove from heat immediately and set flour aside on a sheet of foil or waxed paper.

2. Coat dutch oven with a low-calorie cooking spray. Over high heat, brown meat side of chicken, about 2 minutes. Turn chicken over, reduce heat to medium-high, and add celery, onion, and garlic. Cook 2 minutes longer. Add black pepper, thyme, chicken bouillon granules, and water. Stir in flour with a whisk and blend well.

3. Add potatoes and salt, and bring to a boil. Reduce heat, cover tightly, and simmer 35–40 minutes, or until chicken is tender.

Variation: For a thicker stew, after completing step 3, combine 1 tablespoon cornstarch with 2 tablespoons cold water. Stir into pot and cook 2–3 minutes longer.

MAKE-AHEAD MEAL DIRECTIONS

To Freeze: Complete steps 1–3, omitting potatoes. At end of cooking time, add potatoes and let mixture cool completely. Place mixture in a 1-gallon freezer bag. Seal the bag tightly, allowing no excess air to remain, and freeze. This can be kept frozen for up to 1 month.

To Prepare for Serving: Let chicken and vegetable mixture thaw completely. Pour into dutch oven and cover tightly. Over medium heat, cook about 40 minutes, or until potatoes are tender.

CURRY-RUBBED CHICKEN WITH ACORN SQUASH

Serves 4

Approximately 4.1 g fat, 233 mg sodium per serving

½ teaspoon curry powder
½ teaspoon paprika
¼ teaspoon salt (if desired)
⅛ teaspoon garlic powder
⅛ teaspoon ground ginger
⅛ teaspoon cayenne pepper
⅛ teaspoon black pepper
4 6-ounce skinless chicken breast
   halves, all fat removed
2 tablespoons dark brown sugar,
   packed
1 teaspoon orange zest
½ teaspoon cinnamon
⅛ teaspoon nutmeg
Pinch ground cloves
2 acorn squash (about 1 pound
   each), halved and seeded
Low-calorie cooking spray

1. Preheat oven to 350° F.
2. In a small bowl, combine curry, paprika, salt, garlic powder, ginger, cayenne, and black pepper. Mix well. Rub mixture into chicken and set aside in refrigerator.
3. In a separate small bowl, combine sugar, orange zest, cinnamon, nutmeg, and cloves. Mix well and spoon equal amounts into squash halves.
4. Coat a broiler rack with a low-calorie cooking spray. Place squash on broiler rack and bake 30 minutes. Place chicken on rack with squash and bake 30 minutes longer, or until chicken is done.

MAKE-AHEAD MEAL DIRECTIONS

To Freeze: Complete steps 2–3 of the recipe. (Note: Do not continue to step 4.) Place chicken and squash in two 8-inch square foil pans. Wrap tightly with freezer wrap or freezer foil, and freeze. This can be kept frozen for up to 1 month.

To Prepare for Serving: Let chicken and squash thaw completely. Preheat oven to 350° F. Complete step 4.

LEMON CHICKEN FUSILLI

Serves 4

Approximately 7.9 g fat, 339 mg sodium per serving

Low-calorie cooking spray
¾ pound chicken breast meat, cut
    into 1-inch pieces
1 tablespoon extra-virgin olive oil
1 garlic clove, minced
1 green bell pepper, sliced
1 cup chopped yellow onion
2 cups quartered fresh mushrooms
3 tablespoons fresh lemon juice
½ teaspoon dried dill weed
¼ teaspoon dried oregano leaves
½ teaspoon salt (if desired)
¼ teaspoon freshly ground black
    pepper
3 cups hot cooked fusilli
    (corkscrew pasta) (6 ounces dry)
    (no salt added during cooking)

1. Coat a 10-inch nonstick skillet with a low-calorie cooking spray. Heat 1 minute over medium-high heat. Add chicken and brown 5 minutes, stirring frequently. Remove chicken with a slotted spoon and set aside.

2. To any remaining pan drippings, add olive oil, garlic, green pepper, onion, and mushrooms, and sauté 5 minutes. Add chicken, lemon juice, dill, oregano, salt, and black pepper. Heat thoroughly.

3. Place hot fusilli on a serving platter and spoon chicken mixture over all.

MAKE-AHEAD MEAL DIRECTIONS

To Freeze: Complete steps 1–2 of the recipe. (Note: Do not continue to step 3.) Place chicken mixture in an 8-inch square foil pan. Let cool completely, wrap tightly with freezer foil, and freeze. This can be kept frozen for up to 1 month.

To Prepare for Serving: Let mixture thaw completely. Preheat oven to 350° F. Place wrapped container in oven and bake for 30 minutes, or until heated thoroughly. Place hot fusilli on a serving platter and spoon chicken mixture over all.

CHICKEN TETRAZZINI

Serves 4   Approximately 6.6 g fat, 457 mg sodium per serving

Chicken, pasta, and pimiento tossed in a light cream sauce and topped with cheese.

1½ quarts water
3 5½-ounce skinless chicken breast halves, all fat removed
⅓ cup chopped celery
2 garlic cloves, minced
5 ounces uncooked vermicelli, broken in half
½ cup chopped yellow onion
½ cup chopped green bell pepper
2 cups sliced fresh mushrooms
½ cup evaporated skim milk
¼ cup skim milk
2 tablespoons flour
½ teaspoon chicken bouillon granules
¼ teaspoon freshly ground black pepper
¼ teaspoon salt (if desired)
1 2-ounce jar pimientos, undrained
½ cup (2 ounces) shredded low-sodium, reduced-fat cheddar cheese

1. Preheat oven to 350° F.
2. Bring water to boil in an ovenproof dutch oven. Add chicken, celery, and garlic. Return to boil. Reduce heat and simmer, uncovered, for 12 minutes. Add vermicelli, onion, green pepper, and mushrooms. Return to boil, reduce heat, and simmer 15–17 minutes longer.
3. Remove pot from heat. Remove chicken with slotted spoon. Debone, chop, and set aside. Stir in evaporated and skim milk, and whisk in flour and chicken bouillon granules. Add chicken. Over medium heat, cook until slightly thickened, about 3 minutes. Add black pepper, salt, and pimientos.
4. Bake for 20 minutes. Top with cheese and bake 5 minutes more, or until cheese is melted.

Variation: Instead of the cheddar cheese, use 3 tablespoons grated Parmesan cheese. Omit last 5 minutes of baking. This substitution will reduce the fat content to 5.3 grams per serving and increase the sodium to 492 milligrams per serving.

MAKE-AHEAD MEAL DIRECTIONS

To Freeze: Complete steps 2–3 of the recipe. (Note: Do not continue to step 4.) Place chicken mixture in an 8-inch square foil pan. Let cool completely, wrap tightly with freezer foil, and freeze. This can be frozen for up to 1 month.

To Prepare for Serving: Let mixture thaw completely. Preheat oven to 350° F. Place wrapped container in oven and bake for 40 minutes. Top with cheddar cheese and bake uncovered for 5 minutes.

CHICKEN BRIE

Serves 4   **Approximately 8.9 g fat, 452 mg sodium per serving**

Chicken in a delicate cheese sauce, served with tender asparagus and mushrooms.

Low-calorie cooking spray
14 ounces chicken breast meat, cut
    into bite-sized pieces
¼ teaspoon salt (if desired)
⅛ teaspoon freshly ground black
    pepper
1 teaspoon vegetable oil
½ pound fresh mushrooms,
    quartered
1 garlic clove, minced
¼ cup water
2 cups 2-inch-long pieces fresh
    asparagus
1½ cups skim milk
¼ cup evaporated skim milk
2 tablespoons flour
2¼ ounces peeled ripened Brie
    cheese, cut into ½-inch cubes
1 tablespoon dry white wine
Cracked black pepper

1. Coat a 10-inch nonstick skillet with a low-calorie cooking spray. Heat skillet. Cook chicken over medium heat 8–10 minutes or until chicken is done and almost all liquid has evaporated. Sprinkle chicken with ¼ teaspoon salt and pepper. Place in individual au gratin dishes or on a serving platter. Cover and keep warm.

2. Add oil to remaining pan drippings and heat over medium-high heat. Sauté mushrooms and garlic about 5 minutes. Add to chicken and toss; keep warm. Add water to skillet and bring to boil. Add asparagus. Cover tightly, reduce heat, and simmer about 4 minutes or until tender. Drain well. Place asparagus on paper towels to remove any excess moisture. Wipe skillet dry with a paper towel. Arrange asparagus around chicken and mushrooms.

3. In the same skillet, bring skim milk to a low boil over medium heat. Stir in evaporated milk and whisk in flour. Mix well. Cook, stirring with a flat spatula, until thickened, about 4–5 minutes. Remove skillet from heat, and add Brie and wine. Stir until melted. Pour sauce over chicken and vegetables.

4. Before serving, sprinkle with remaining ¼ teaspoon salt and lightly with cracked black pepper.

MAKE-AHEAD MEAL DIRECTIONS

To Freeze: Complete step 1 of the recipe, except spread chicken in an 8-inch square foil pan. Complete steps 2–3. (Note: Do not continue to step 4.) Let casserole cool completely, wrap tightly with freezer foil, and freeze. This can be kept frozen for up to 2 weeks.

To Prepare for Serving: Let mixture thaw completely. Preheat oven to 350° F. Unwrap container and bake for 30 minutes, until all ingredients are heated thoroughly. Before serving, sprinkle with remaining ¼ teaspoon salt and lightly with cracked black pepper.

HOME-STYLE CHICKEN AND RICE

Serves 4

Approximately 2.9 g fat, 446 mg sodium per serving

1 quart water
1 garlic clove, minced
3 5½-ounce skinless chicken breast
  halves, all fat removed
⅔ cup uncooked white rice
½ cup chopped celery
½ cup chopped yellow onion
½ teaspoon chicken bouillon
  granules
¼ teaspoon freshly ground black
  pepper
2 tablespoons chopped fresh
  parsley
1 large bay leaf
¼ teaspoon salt (if desired)

1. Bring water to a boil in a 2-quart saucepan. Add garlic and chicken, and return to a boil. Reduce heat, cover tightly, and simmer 30 minutes.

2. Remove chicken from pot, debone, and set aside. Add rice to broth with onion, celery, chicken bouillon granules, black pepper, parsley, and bay leaf. Simmer covered for 20 minutes.

3. Add chicken and salt. Remove from heat. Let stand 5 minutes, uncovered. Remove bay leaf before serving.

MAKE-AHEAD MEAL DIRECTIONS

To Freeze: Complete steps 1–3 of the recipe. Place mixture in an 8-inch square foil pan. Let cool completely, wrap tightly with freezer foil, and freeze. This can be kept frozen for up to 1 month.

To Prepare for Serving: Let mixture thaw completely. Preheat oven to 350° F. Place wrapped container in oven and bake for 45–50 minutes, or until heated thoroughly.

LEMON CHICKEN WITH ARTICHOKES

Serves 4   **Approximately 9.6 g fat, 479 mg sodium per serving**

Chicken seasoned with Italian herbs and fresh lemon, tossed with artichokes, black olives, and onions, and topped with Parmesan cheese.

¼ cup fresh lemon juice
2 tablespoons extra-virgin olive oil
2 garlic cloves, minced
½ teaspoon dried oregano leaves
¼ teaspoon dried basil leaves
½ teaspoon dry mustard
¼ teaspoon black pepper
¾ pound chicken breast meat, cut into bite-sized pieces
2 cups cooked egg or spinach noodles (about 4 ounces dry) (no salt or margarine added during cooking)
4 canned artichoke hearts, quartered
8 medium-sized black olives, thinly sliced
2 tablespoons minced yellow onion
¼ teaspoon salt (if desired)
1 tablespoon grated Parmesan cheese

1. In a 1-quart freezer bag, combine lemon juice, olive oil, garlic, oregano, basil, dry mustard, and black pepper. Mix well and add chicken. Seal bag, releasing any excess air. Shake to coat chicken thoroughly. Marinate in the refrigerator overnight or at least 2 hours.
2. Preheat oven to 350° F.
3. Place cooked noodles in a 2-quart casserole dish. Toss with chicken, marinade, artichoke hearts, black olives, and onion. Cover and bake for 40 minutes, stirring midway. Add salt and blend thoroughly. Top with Parmesan cheese and serve.

MAKE-AHEAD MEAL DIRECTIONS

To Freeze: Prepare marinade and coat chicken according to step 1 of the recipe. Freeze instead of marinating. (Note: Do not continue to step 2.) This can be kept frozen for up to 1 month.

To Prepare for Serving: Let chicken and marinade thaw completely. Shake to blend seasonings. Complete steps 2–3 of the recipe.

THE BAGGED BIRD

Serves 4   Approximately 5.7 g fat, 493 mg sodium per serving

Chicken and hearty vegetables baked in a browning bag for exceptional flavor and tenderness.

1 tablespoon flour
1 medium browning bag
4 medium carrots, peeled and cut into 3-inch pieces
2 medium yellow onions, quartered
2 celery stalks, cut into 3-inch pieces
½ medium cabbage, cut into 4 wedges
½ thinly sliced green bell pepper
4 6-ounce skinless chicken breast halves, all fat removed
½ teaspoon chicken bouillon granules
½ teaspoon paprika
¼ teaspoon poultry seasoning
⅜ teaspoon salt (if desired)
¼ teaspoon black pepper

1. Preheat oven to 350° F.
2. Place flour in browning bag and shake well. Place the carrots, onions, celery, cabbage, and green pepper in bag. Place the chicken pieces on top of the vegetables. In a small bowl, combine chicken bouillon granules, paprika, poultry seasoning, salt, and black pepper. Mix well and sprinkle over all. Secure bag tightly with tie.
3. Place bag in a 8″ × 12″ baking pan. Make 6½-inch slits in top of bag. Bake about 1 hour and 15 minutes. Carefully remove wrapping and arrange chicken and vegetables on a serving platter.

MAKE-AHEAD MEAL DIRECTIONS

To Freeze: Complete step 2, omitting cabbage. (Note: Do not continue to step 3.) Tightly wrap bagged chicken and vegetables in freezer foil for extra protection. Freeze. This can be kept frozen for up to 1 month.

To Prepare for Serving: Let chicken and vegetables thaw completely. Preheat oven to 350° F. Remove foil, open bag, and add cabbage. Secure bag tightly with tie. Complete step 3.

JALAPEÑO-LIME CHICKEN

Serves 4

Approximately 8.1 g fat, 390 mg sodium per serving

⅓ cup lime juice

1½ teaspoons barbecue smoke seasoning (I use Liquid Smoke)

1 tablespoon plus 1 teaspoon extra-virgin olive oil

½ teaspoon cumin

½ teaspoon salt (if desired)

¼ teaspoon paprika

4 small jalapeño peppers, thinly sliced with seeds in (see Note)

4 6-ounce skinless chicken breast halves, all fat removed

Low-calorie cooking spray

2 cups hot cooked rice

1 medium tomato, seeded and chopped

2 tablespoons chopped fresh parsley

¼ teaspoon ground turmeric

1. In a 1-gallon freezer bag, combine lime juice, smoke seasoning, olive oil, cumin, salt, paprika, and peppers. Mix well and add chicken. Seal bag, releasing any excess air. Shake to coat chicken thoroughly. Marinate in the refrigerator overnight or at least 2 hours, turning bag occasionally.

2. Preheat broiler.

3. Coat a broiler rack with a low-calorie cooking spray. Place chicken on rack. Spoon half the marinade over the chicken. Broil 2–3 inches away from heat source for 3 minutes. Turn and spoon the remaining marinade over chicken. Broil 3 minutes more or until chicken is done.

4. Toss hot rice with tomato, parsley, and turmeric. Spoon onto center of a serving platter, and arrange chicken around rice. Serve immediately.

Note: The jalapeño seeds make for a rather hot dish. If you prefer a less fiery meal, omit the seeds.

MAKE-AHEAD MEAL DIRECTIONS

To Freeze: Prepare marinade and coat chicken according to step 1 of the recipe. Freeze instead of marinating. (Note: Do not continue to step 2.) This can be kept frozen for up to 1 month.

To Prepare for Serving: Let chicken and marinade thaw completely. Shake to blend seasonings. Complete steps 2–4 of the recipe.

COUNTRY CHICKEN POT PIES

Serves 4

Approximately 9.8 g fat, 490 mg sodium per serving

1 tablespoon plus 1 teaspoon
   unsalted butter
1 10-ounce can low-sodium
   chicken broth
⅔ cup skim milk
¾ teaspoon chicken bouillon
   granules
½ cup plus 4 teaspoons flour,
   divided
1½ cups chopped cooked chicken
1⅓ cups frozen mixed vegetables
1 6-ounce potato, peeled and
   diced into ¼-inch cubes
⅓ cup finely chopped celery
3 tablespoons finely chopped
   yellow onion
2 tablespoons chopped fresh
   parsley
½ teaspoon poultry seasoning
⅛ teaspoon black pepper
1 tablespoon vegetable oil
1 tablespoon plus 1 teaspoon
   nonfat buttermilk

1. Preheat oven to 425° F.
2. In a 10-inch nonstick skillet, melt butter over medium-high heat. Add chicken broth, skim milk, and chicken bouillon granules. Whisk in 4 teaspoons flour and bring to a boil. Cook, stirring with a flat spatula, about 4–5 minutes, or until slightly thickened. Remove from heat. Add chicken, mixed vegetables, potato, celery, onion, parsley, poultry seasoning, and black pepper. Divide mixture evenly into 4 individual casserole dishes.
3. Combine ½ cup flour, oil, and buttermilk. Blend well. Divide into 4 balls. Place 1 ball on top of a 12-inch sheet of plastic wrap. Top with another sheet of plastic wrap. Press down with a rolling pin and roll dough out to make a thin individual pie crust. Place crust on top of an individual pot pie. Repeat procedure with remaining dough balls.
4. Bake for 45–55 minutes.

MAKE-AHEAD MEAL DIRECTIONS

To Freeze: Complete step 2, omitting potato and dividing mixture into four 5″ × 3″ foil loaf pans. Let mixture cool. Stir in raw potato. Complete step 3.

Wrap each pie tightly with freezer foil and freeze. These can be kept frozen for up to 1 month.

To Prepare for Serving: Do not thaw. Preheat oven to 425° F. Unwrap frozen pies and bake for 55–60 minutes.

CHICKEN AND STUFFING CASSEROLE

Serves 4

Approximately 9.7 g fat, 363 mg sodium per serving

Low-calorie cooking spray
¾ pound chicken breast meat, cut into bite-sized pieces
½ cup chopped yellow onion
¼ cup finely chopped celery
1 cup corn bread stuffing mix
1 tablespoon corn bread seasoning mix
2 slices reduced-calorie bread, toasted and cubed
1 cup hot water
⅛ teaspoon ground sage
4 tablespoons chopped fresh parsley
½ cup frozen green peas
¾ cup plus 2 tablespoons condensed cream of chicken soup, undiluted
¼ cup buttermilk
1 tablespoon fresh lemon juice
¼ teaspoon freshly ground black pepper
⅛ teaspoon paprika

1. Preheat oven to 350° F.
2. Coat a 10-inch ovenproof nonstick skillet with a low-calorie cooking spray. Heat skillet 1 minute over high heat. Add chicken and brown 2–3 minutes, stirring constantly. Remove chicken from skillet and set aside. Wipe skillet dry with a paper towel. In same skillet, sauté onion and celery over medium heat for about 4 minutes, or until vegetables are tender but still crisp. Add stuffing mix, seasoning mix, cubed toast, hot water, sage, and 2 tablespoons parsley. Mix gently but thoroughly, spreading evenly over bottom of skillet. Top with frozen peas and cooked chicken. In a mixing bowl, combine soup, buttermilk, lemon juice, and black pepper. Blend well and spoon evenly over chicken and peas. Top with remaining 2 tablespoons parsley and sprinkle with paprika.
4. Bake uncovered for 25–30 minutes.
5. Remove from oven and heat broiler. Broil 2–3 inches away from heat source for 1–2 minutes, or until light brown. Let stand 5 minutes before serving.

MAKE-AHEAD MEAL DIRECTIONS

To Freeze: Complete steps 2–3, except spread vegetable and stuffing mixture in bottom of an 8-inch square foil pan. (Note: Do not continue to step 4.) After adding peas, chicken, and sauce, let cool completely. Wrap tightly with freezer foil and freeze. This can be kept frozen for up to 1 month.

To Prepare for Serving: Let mixture thaw completely. Preheat oven to 350° F. Unwrap and bake for 40–45 minutes, or until heated thoroughly. Complete step 5.

ORIENTAL BAKED CHICKEN

Serves 4   **Approximately 4 g fat, 479 mg sodium per serving**

Chicken and vegetables baked with white and wild rice and seasoned with soy sauce.

Low-calorie cooking spray
1 cup plus 2 tablespoons hot water
¾ teaspoon beef bouillon granules
¼ cup uncooked wild rice
⅓ cup uncooked white rice
3 tablespoons chopped pimiento
2 garlic cloves, minced
¼ cup chopped green onion
1 cup sliced fresh mushrooms
½ cup drained and slivered canned
  water chestnuts
2 cups small fresh broccoli
  flowerets
4 5½-ounce skinless chicken breast
  halves, all fat removed
4½ teaspoons low-sodium soy
  sauce
Freshly ground black pepper

1. Preheat oven to 350° F.
2. Coat a 2-quart casserole dish with a low-calorie cooking spray. In the casserole dish, combine water, beef bouillon granules, wild rice, white rice, pimiento, garlic, onion, mushrooms, water chestnuts, and broccoli. Stir well and top with chicken breasts. Drizzle 2½ teaspoons soy sauce over chicken and sprinkle with black pepper.
3. Cover tightly and bake for 50–60 minutes, or until rice is done. Remove from oven and heat broiler.
4. Uncover casserole, remove chicken, and stir rice mixture. Replace chicken and broil 2–3 inches away from heat source for 1–2 minutes, or until chicken is brown. Remove from oven and sprinkle with the remaining 2 teaspoons soy sauce.

MAKE-AHEAD MEAL DIRECTIONS

To Freeze: Complete step 2, using an 8-inch square foil pan in place of casserole dish. (Note: Do not continue to step 3.) Let mixture cool completely, wrap tightly with freezer foil, and freeze. This can be kept frozen for up to 1 month.

To Prepare for Serving: Let mixture thaw completely. Preheat oven to 350° F. Place wrapped container in oven and bake for 70 minutes, or until rice is done. Remove from oven and heat broiler. Complete step 4 of the recipe.

❧ ⚜ ❧

CHICKEN ENCHILADAS

Serves 4

Approximately 8 g fat, 490 mg sodium per serving

½ pound chicken breast meat, cut into ½-inch pieces
1 teaspoon low-sodium chicken bouillon granules
1 tablespoon plus 1 teaspoon chili powder
2 garlic cloves, minced
½ teaspoon dried oregano leaves
½ teaspoon cumin
1 16-ounce can chopped tomatoes, drained
½ cup chopped yellow onion
½ cup chopped green bell pepper
½ cup finely chopped celery
3 tablespoons chopped fresh parsley
2 tablespoons dry red wine
⅛ teaspoon ground red pepper
½ teaspoon sugar
⅛ teaspoon salt (if desired)
4 6-inch corn tortillas
½ cup (2 ounces) shredded mozzarella cheese
½ cup (2 ounces) grated low-sodium, reduced-fat cheddar cheese
2 jalapeño peppers (if desired), seeded and finely chopped

1. Preheat oven to 350° F.
2. In a 10-inch nonstick skillet, combine chicken, chicken bouillon granules, chili powder, garlic, oregano, cumin, tomatoes, onion, green pepper, celery, parsley, wine, red pepper, sugar, and salt. Bring to a boil, reduce heat, cover tightly, and simmer for 15 minutes. Uncover and cook 5 minutes longer. Remove from skillet and set aside.
3. Wrap tortillas tightly in aluminum foil. Warm in oven for 10 minutes to soften.
4. Keeping the unfilled tortillas wrapped, spread a tortilla with ⅛ of the meat mixture. Roll the tortilla and place in skillet with seam side down. Repeat with remaining tortillas. Top rolled tortillas with remaining half of meat mixture. Sprinkle with cheese and jalapeño peppers, if desired. Bake uncovered for 5–6 minutes, or until cheese melts.

MAKE-AHEAD MEAL DIRECTIONS

To Freeze: Complete step 2 of the recipe. (Note: Do not continue to step 3.) Let chicken mixture cool completely. Place in a 1-quart freezer bag. Seal bag tightly, allowing no excess air to remain, and freeze. This can be kept frozen for up to 1 month.

To Prepare for Serving: Let chicken mixture thaw completely. Preheat oven to 350° F. Warm and fill tortillas as directed in steps 3–4 of the recipe. Without adding cheese, bake uncovered for 20 minutes. Sprinkle with cheese and jalapeño peppers, if desired. Bake uncovered for 6–8 minutes, or until cheese melts.

❧— ❦

PEPPERED CHICKEN AND ONIONS

Serves 4

Approximately 5.7 g fat, 457 mg sodium per serving

Low-calorie cooking spray
4 5½-ounce skinless chicken breast halves, all fat removed
⅔ cup chopped yellow onion
⅓ cup slivered green bell pepper
½ cup uncooked white rice
1 cup hot water
½ teaspoon chicken bouillon granules
¼ teaspoon paprika
⅛ teaspoon freshly ground black pepper
⅛ teaspoon garlic powder
⅜ teaspoon salt
2 teaspoons butter or margarine
2 tablespoons chopped fresh parsley
½ teaspoon lemon pepper

1. Preheat oven to 350° F.

2. Coat a 10-inch ovenproof nonstick skillet with a low-calorie cooking spray. Over high heat, brown meat side of chicken breasts 1 minute. Remove chicken and set aside.

3. In the same skillet, sauté onion and green pepper, quickly tossing until edges begin to brown, about 2–3 minutes. Remove from heat. Add rice and water to vegetables in skillet. Top with chicken. Sprinkle with chicken bouillon granules, paprika, black pepper, garlic powder, and ¼ teaspoon salt. Place a ½-teaspoon pat of cold butter or margarine on top of each chicken breast. Sprinkle with parsley.

4. Cover tightly and bake for 50–60 minutes, or until rice is done. Remove from oven and heat broiler.

5. Uncover skillet, remove chicken, and stir rice mixture. Replace chicken and sprinkle with remaining ⅛ teaspoon salt and lemon pepper. Broil 2–3 inches away from heat source for 1–2 minutes, or until chicken is brown.

MAKE-AHEAD MEAL DIRECTIONS

To Freeze: Complete steps 2–3 of the recipe. (Note: Do not continue to step 4.) Let cool completely. Cover skillet tightly with freezer foil and freeze. This can be kept frozen for up to 1 month.

To Prepare for Serving: Let chicken and vegetables thaw completely. Preheat oven to 350° F. Place wrapped skillet in oven and bake for 70 minutes, or until rice is done. Remove from oven and heat broiler. Complete step 5 of the recipe.

❈ ❈

ROSEMARY CHICKEN WITH RICE

Serves 4   **Approximately 7 g fat, 436 mg sodium per serving**

Tender herbed chicken, baked with just a hint of lemon and olive oil and served over rice.

Low-calorie cooking spray
1 cup hot water
½ teaspoon chicken bouillon
   granules
½ cup uncooked white rice
½ cup finely chopped yellow onion
½ teaspoon salt (if desired)
4 5½-ounce skinless chicken breast
   halves, all fat removed
2 tablespoons fresh lemon juice
1 tablespoon extra-virgin olive oil
½ teaspoon dried rosemary leaves
⅛ teaspoon garlic powder
⅛ teaspoon freshly ground black
   pepper
⅛ teaspoon paprika

1. Preheat oven to 350° F.
2. Coat a 2-quart casserole dish with a low-calorie cooking spray. In the casserole dish, combine water, chicken bouillon granules, rice, onion, and ¼ teaspoon salt. Stir well and top with chicken breasts. Drizzle lemon juice and olive oil over chicken. Sprinkle with rosemary, garlic powder, black pepper, and paprika.
3. Cover tightly and bake for 50–60 minutes, or until rice is done. Remove casserole from oven and heat broiler.
4. Uncover casserole, remove chicken, and stir rice mixture. Replace chicken and sprinkle with remaining ¼ teaspoon salt. Broil 2–3 inches away from heat source for 1–2 minutes, or until chicken is brown.

MAKE-AHEAD MEAL DIRECTIONS

To Freeze: Complete step 2, using an 8-inch square foil pan in place of the casserole dish. (Note: Do not continue to step 3.) Wrap tightly with freezer foil and freeze. This can be kept frozen for up to 1 month.

To Prepare for Serving: Let chicken thaw completely. Preheat oven to 350° F. Place wrapped container in oven and bake for 70 minutes, or until rice is done. Remove pan from oven and heat broiler. Complete step 4 of the recipe.

CHICKEN WITH HERBED COUNTRY MUSTARD ON HOT FRENCH BREAD

Serves 4

Approximately 6.3 g fat, 316 mg sodium per serving

¼ cup country-style or plain Dijon mustard
¼ cup finely chopped red onion
½ teaspoon dried tarragon leaves
10–12 drops hot sauce
2 teaspoons fresh lime juice
4 4-ounce boneless chicken breast halves, all fat removed
Low-calorie cooking spray
4 1½-ounce French bread rolls, split
4 lettuce leaves
1 large tomato, cut in 4 slices
Freshly ground black pepper

1. Preheat broiler.
2. In a small mixing bowl, combine mustard, onion, tarragon, hot sauce, and lime juice. Mix well. Flatten chicken breasts to ¼-inch thickness, being careful not to tear. Spread mustard mixture evenly over top of each chicken breast.
3. Coat a broiler rack with a low-calorie cooking spray. Broil chicken at least 5 inches away from heat source for 5 minutes. Do not turn. During the last 2 minutes of broiling time, place rolls on lower oven rack to warm.
4. On warmed rolls, layer chicken, lettuce leaves, and tomato slices. Sprinkle with freshly ground pepper. Serve immediately.

MAKE-AHEAD MEAL DIRECTIONS

To Freeze: Complete step 2 of the recipe. (Note: Do not continue to step 3.) Place in single layer on cookie sheet and freeze, then place in a 1-gallon freezer bag. Seal bag tightly, allowing no excess air to remain, and freeze. The chicken can be kept frozen for up to 1 month.

For convenience, rolls also freeze well for up to 2 weeks.

To Prepare for Serving: Let chicken thaw completely. Preheat broiler. Complete steps 3–4 of the recipe.

EUNICE'S CHILI CHICKEN STEW

Serves 4 **Approximately 3.6 g fat, 440 mg sodium per serving**

Chicken, tomatoes, and other vegetables stewed with Mexican seasonings, served with rice, and topped with sour cream and onions.

Low-calorie cooking spray
½ pound chicken breast meat, cut into bite-sized pieces
1½ cups chopped yellow onion
¾ cup chopped green bell pepper
½ cup chopped celery
2 garlic cloves, minced
3 cups canned no-salt chopped tomatoes, undrained
⅔ cup drained canned pinto beans
¼ cup plus 1 tablespoon hot picante sauce
1½ teaspoons chili powder
¾ teaspoon cumin
2 cups cooked rice (no margarine or salt added during cooking)
¼ cup light sour cream
¼ cup chopped green onion

1. Coat a dutch oven, preferably cast-iron, with a low-calorie cooking spray. Over high heat, sauté chicken, onion, green pepper, celery, and garlic until lightly browned, about 5–7 minutes. Add tomatoes and liquid, beans, picante sauce, chili powder, and cumin. Reduce heat, cover tightly, and simmer 25–30 minutes.

2. Place ½ cup rice in each of 4 individual bowls. Spoon ¼ of the chicken stew over each serving of rice. Top each with 1 tablespoon sour cream and 1 tablespoon green onion. Serve immediately.

MAKE-AHEAD MEAL DIRECTIONS

To Freeze: Complete step 1 of the recipe. (Note: Do not continue to step 2.) Let stew cool completely. Place in a 1-gallon freezer bag. Seal bag tightly, allowing no excess air to remain, and freeze. This can be kept frozen for up to 1 month.

To Prepare for Serving: Let stew thaw completely. Pour into a medium saucepan and heat thoroughly over medium heat. Complete step 2 of the recipe.

❖ ❖

SATURDAY NIGHT TACOS

Serves 4

Approximately 5.2 g fat, 420 mg sodium per serving

8 corn taco shells
2 cups chopped cooked chicken
2 tablespoons chili powder
½ teaspoon cumin
2 garlic cloves, minced
¼ teaspoon freshly ground black
    pepper
½ cup water
2 cups shredded lettuce
2 medium tomatoes, chopped
½ cup finely chopped yellow onion
⅓ cup prepared hot salsa

1. Place taco shells in a warm oven.
2. In a 10-inch nonstick skillet, over medium heat, combine chicken, chili powder, cumin, garlic, black pepper, and water. Cover and simmer 5 minutes.
3. Spoon chicken mixture into taco shells. Top each with lettuce, tomato, onion, and salsa (about 2 teaspoons each).

MAKE-AHEAD MEAL DIRECTIONS

To Freeze: Complete step 2 of the recipe. (Note: Do not continue to step 3.) Let chicken mixture cool completely. Place in a 1-quart freezer bag. Seal the bag tightly, allowing no excess air to remain, and freeze. This can be kept frozen for up to 1 month.

To Prepare for Serving: Let chicken mixture thaw completely. Place taco shells in a warm oven. Pour chicken mixture into a saucepan and heat thoroughly over moderate heat, stirring frequently. Fill taco shells as directed in step 3.

BARBECUED-CHICKEN TORTILLAS

Serves 4

Approximately 5.9 g fat, 456 mg sodium per serving

1½ cups shredded cooked chicken
3 tablespoons barbecue sauce
¼ cup reduced-calorie low-sodium catsup
1 teaspoon dry red wine
1 garlic clove, minced
⅓ cup finely chopped yellow onion
⅛ teaspoon hot sauce
⅛ teaspoon dry mustard
¼ teaspoon barbecue smoke seasoning (I use Liquid Smoke)
⅛ teaspoon freshly ground black pepper
4 6-inch flour tortillas
¼ cup light sour cream
¼ cup chopped green onions
½ teaspoon chili powder

1. In a 1-quart saucepan, combine chicken, barbecue sauce, catsup, wine, garlic, onion, hot sauce, dry mustard, smoke seasoning, and black pepper. Bring to a boil, reduce heat, cover tightly, and simmer 3 minutes.

2. Spoon ¼ of the mixture over each tortilla. Top with 1 tablespoon sour cream, 1 tablespoon green onion, and ⅛ teaspoon chili powder. Serve open-face or rolled.

MAKE-AHEAD MEAL DIRECTIONS

To Freeze: Complete step 1 of the recipe. (Note: Do not continue to step 2.) Let chicken mixture cool completely. Place in a 1-quart freezer bag. Seal bag tightly, allowing no excess air to remain, and freeze. This can be kept frozen for up to 1 month.

To Prepare for Serving: Let chicken mixture thaw completely. Pour chicken mixture into a saucepan, cover, and heat thoroughly over medium heat. Fill tortillas as directed in step 2.

❧ ❧

SMOKED BLACK BEAN, RED PEPPER, AND CHICKEN STEW

Serves 4

Approximately 3.5 g fat, 495 mg sodium per serving

1 cup dried black beans
2 quarts water
Low-calorie cooking spray
4 garlic cloves, minced
½ pound chicken breast meat, cut into 1-inch pieces
⅔ cup (about 3 ounces) chopped turkey ham
¾ teaspoon barbecue smoke seasoning (I use Liquid Smoke)
2 large red bell peppers, sliced
1 cup chopped yellow onion
3 jalapeño peppers, seeded and minced
⅛ teaspoon ground red pepper
⅛ teaspoon freshly ground black pepper
1½ teaspoons dried oregano leaves
1 teaspoon low-sodium chicken bouillon granules
1 tablespoon Dijon mustard
⅜ teaspoon salt (if desired)
¼ cup chopped fresh parsley
½ cup finely chopped white onion

1. Rinse beans in cold water. Combine with 1 quart cold water in a dutch oven, preferably cast-iron. Bring to a boil, reduce heat, cover tightly, and simmer 2 minutes. Remove from heat and let stand 1 hour. Drain and rinse beans. Wipe dutch oven dry with a paper towel.

2. Coat dutch oven with a low-calorie cooking spray. Over medium-high heat, add garlic, chicken, turkey ham, and ½ teaspoon smoke seasoning. Sauté 3–4 minutes, remove from pot, and set aside.

3. Liberally add more low-calorie cooking spray. Over medium-high heat, add red peppers, onion, jalapeño peppers, ground red pepper, black pepper, oregano, and chicken bouillon granules. Sauté 10 minutes, stirring frequently. Add remaining 1 quart water and beans. Bring to a boil, reduce heat, cover tightly, and simmer 2 hours. Stir in chicken, turkey ham, mustard, salt, and remaining ¼ teaspoon smoke seasoning. Cook, covered, 8–10 minutes longer.

4. To improve flavor, you may refrigerate overnight, then reheat. Top each serving with 1 tablespoon fresh parsley and 2 tablespoons onion.

MAKE-AHEAD MEAL DIRECTIONS

To Freeze: Complete steps 1–3 of the recipe. (Note: Do not continue to step 4.) Let stew cool completely. Place in two 1-gallon freezer bags. Seal the bag tightly, allowing no excess air to remain, and freeze. This can be kept frozen for up to 1 month.

To Prepare for Serving: Let stew thaw completely. Pour into dutch oven, cover, and heat thoroughly over moderate heat, stirring occasionally. Top each serving with 1 tablespoon fresh parsley and 2 tablespoons onion.

CHICKEN MOZZARELLA

Serves 4   **Approximately 6.2 g fat, 434 mg sodium per serving**

Chicken breasts baked in a mildly seasoned tomato sauce and topped with mozzarella cheese.

2 cups tender-cooked spaghetti (no oil or salt added during cooking)
Low-calorie cooking spray
1 pound chicken breast meat, cut into bite-sized pieces
¾ cup tomato sauce
1 cup thinly sliced fresh mushrooms
¼ cup thinly sliced green bell pepper
¼ cup finely chopped yellow onion
¼ teaspoon garlic powder
¼ teaspoon dried basil leaves
½ teaspoon dried oregano leaves
¼ teaspoon freshly ground black pepper
⅛ teaspoon fennel seeds
½ teaspoon low-sodium Worcestershire sauce
2 tablespoons chopped fresh parsley
1-2 tablespoons dry red wine
½ cup (2 ounces) shredded mozzarella cheese
1 tablespoon freshly grated Parmesan cheese

1. Preheat oven to 350° F.
2. Rinse spaghetti in cold water and drain well. Spread in bottom of an 8-inch square baking dish coated with a low-calorie cooking spray. Flatten chicken breasts to ¼-inch thickness and place on top of spaghetti.
3. In a mixing bowl, combine tomato sauce with mushrooms, bell pepper, onion, garlic powder, basil, oregano, black pepper, fennel seeds, Worcestershire sauce, parsley, and wine. Mix well and spoon over chicken and spaghetti.
4. Bake, uncovered, for 30 minutes. Top with mozzarella cheese and bake 8-10 minutes longer, or until cheese melts. Sprinkle with Parmesan cheese.

MAKE-AHEAD MEAL DIRECTIONS

To Freeze: Complete steps 2-3 of the recipe, using an 8-inch square foil pan in place of the baking dish. (Note: Do not continue to step 4.) Let mixture cool completely, wrap tightly with freezer foil, and freeze. This can be kept frozen for up to 1 month.

To Prepare for Serving: Let mixture thaw completely. Preheat oven to 350° F. Place wrapped container in oven and bake for 40-45 minutes, or until chicken is tender. Top with mozzarella cheese and bake 8-10 minutes longer, or until cheese melts. Sprinkle with Parmesan cheese.

TARRAGON BUTTERED CHICKEN

Serves 4

Approximately 9.0 g fat, 457 mg sodium per serving

4 6-ounce boneless chicken
   breasts, all fat removed
3 tablespoons low-calorie
   margarine
2 teaspoons white wine vinegar
1 green onion, finely chopped
2 teaspoons finely chopped fresh
   parsley
½ teaspoon dried tarragon leaves
½ teaspoon salt (if desired)
¾ cup water
3 cups cauliflower flowerets
Low-calorie cooking spray
Freshly ground black pepper
   (if desired)

1. Flatten chicken breasts to ¼-inch thickness. In a small mixing bowl, combine margarine with vinegar, green onion, parsley, tarragon, and ¼ teaspoon salt. Mix until well blended, and shape mixture into 4 balls.

2. In a 10-inch nonstick skillet, bring water to a boil. Add cauliflower. Reduce heat, cover tightly, and simmer 4 minutes, or until tender but still crisp. Remove cauliflower and drain well. Cover and keep warm. Wipe skillet dry with a paper towel.

3. Coat the skillet with a low-calorie cooking spray and heat over medium-high heat. Add chicken and sauté 3 minutes. Turn and sauté 2½ minutes longer or until cooked.

4. Remove skillet from heat. Place herb balls on top of chicken and arrange cauliflower around chicken. Cover and let stand 2 minutes, allowing margarine to melt over all. Sprinkle with black pepper.

MAKE-AHEAD MEAL DIRECTIONS

To Freeze: Complete step 1 of the recipe. (Note: Do not continue to step 2.) Place chicken and herb balls in a single layer on a cookie sheet and freeze overnight. Transfer to a 1-gallon freezer bag. This can be kept frozen for up to 1 month.

To Prepare for Serving: Let chicken and herb balls thaw completely in the refrigerator. Complete steps 2–4 of the recipe.

HERBED BREADED CHICKEN

Serves 4   **Approximately 9.6 g fat, 302 mg sodium per serving**

Chicken nuggets coated with Dijon mustard, herbs, and bread crumbs, and baked until tender.

1 cup water
2 cups fresh cauliflower flowerets
2 cups diagonally sliced carrots
¼ teaspoon nutmeg
¼ teaspoon ground ginger
½ teaspoon sugar
⅛ teaspoon salt (if desired)
1 tablespoon plus 1 teaspoon
   Dijon mustard
2 tablespoons unsalted butter,
   melted and cooled
1 pound chicken breast meat, cut
   into bite-sized pieces
4 slices reduced-calorie bread,
   toasted and grated
1 tablespoon chopped fresh
   parsley
½ teaspoon dried tarragon leaves
¼ teaspoon freshly ground black
   pepper
⅛ teaspoon paprika
Low-calorie cooking spray

1. Preheat oven to 475° F.
2. Bring water to a boil in a 12-inch ovenproof nonstick skillet. Add cauliflower, carrots, nutmeg, ginger, sugar, and salt. Cover tightly, reduce heat, and simmer 5–8 minutes or until vegetables are tender but still crisp. Remove cauliflower and carrots, drain well, and set aside. Wipe skillet dry with a paper towel.
3. In a small bowl, combine mustard and 2 tablespoons butter. Toss chicken with butter mixture until thoroughly coated. In a separate bowl, combine bread crumbs, parsley, tarragon, black pepper, and paprika. Mix well. Dredge mustard-coated chicken in bread crumb mixture.
4. Liberally coat skillet with a low-calorie cooking spray. Place chicken in skillet and bake uncovered for 6 minutes. Turn pieces and arrange cauliflower and carrots around outer edges of skillet. Bake 6 minutes longer and serve immediately.

Do Not Freeze

THE ALL-AMERICAN BASKET

Serves 4   **Approximately 7.1 g fat, 381 mg sodium per serving**

Oven-fried chicken and home fries, served in napkin-lined straw baskets.

8 3-ounce chicken drumsticks,
  skin and fat removed
½ cup nonfat buttermilk
½ cup flour
½ teaspoon salt (if desired)
⅛ teaspoon freshly ground black
  pepper
¼ teaspoon poultry seasoning
⅛ teaspoon garlic powder
Low-calorie cooking spray
2 6-ounce potatoes, unpeeled, cut
  into 3″ × ¼″ wedges
1 teaspoon vegetable oil
Paprika

1. Preheat oven to 400° F.
2. Coat drumsticks with buttermilk. In a small mixing bowl, combine flour, ¼ teaspoon salt, black pepper, poultry seasoning, and garlic powder. Mix well. Place chicken on a sheet of waxed paper. Sift half of the flour mixture over chicken. Turn chicken and sift with remaining flour mixture to cover evenly.
3. Coat a large nonstick cookie sheet liberally with a low-calorie cooking spray. Place chicken on cookie sheet. Bake for 30 minutes. Turn pieces and bake 5 more minutes.
4. While chicken is baking, toss potatoes thoroughly with oil. Place on a cookie sheet and bake with chicken for 6 minutes. With a flat spatula, turn potatoes, sprinkle with paprika and remaining ¼ teaspoon salt, and bake 6 minutes longer. Remove chicken and potatoes from oven. Place 2 drumsticks and ¼ of the fries in each of 4 napkin-lined baskets.

Do Not Freeze

❧ ❧

SICILIAN CHICKEN WITH PASTA

Serves 4   **Approximately 9.9 g fat, 296 mg sodium per serving**

Tender chicken baked with olives, garlic, olive oil, and wine and served with linguine.

4 4-ounce skinless chicken breast halves, all fat removed
3 tablespoons finely chopped fresh parsley
1 tablespoon plus 1 teaspoon extra-virgin olive oil
1 tablespoon plus 1 teaspoon white vinegar
1 tablespoon dry white wine
1 tablespoon capers, drained and chopped
½ teaspoon dried oregano leaves
¼ teaspoon black pepper
1 tablespoon minced yellow onion
12 medium-sized black olives, pitted and finely chopped
¼ teaspoon garlic powder
⅛ teaspoon salt (if desired)
2 cups hot cooked linguine (about 4 ounces dry)
2 tablespoons grated Parmesan cheese
Lemon wedges

1. Flatten chicken to ¼-inch thickness. In a mixing bowl, combine parsley, olive oil, vinegar, wine, capers, oregano, black pepper, onion, olives, garlic powder, and salt. Mix well and spoon evenly over chicken. Marinate overnight or at least 2 hours.

2. Preheat oven to 350° F.

3. Place chicken and marinade in an 8-inch square baking dish. Bake uncovered 18–20 minutes, or until cooked.

4. Place on a serving platter. Arrange linguine around chicken and sprinkle pasta with Parmesan cheese. Serve immediately with fresh lemon wedges.

Do Not Freeze

❧ ❧

BARBECUED CHICKEN–STUFFED POTATOES

Serves 4

Approximately 4.3 g fat, 479 mg sodium per serving

4 7-ounce baking potatoes
½ cup hickory-smoked barbecue
   sauce
2 teaspoons dry red wine
½ pound chicken breast meat, cut
   into bite-sized pieces
1 large red or green bell pepper,
   cut into 1-inch pieces
½ cup (2 ounces) grated low-
   sodium, reduced-fat sharp
   cheddar cheese
¼ cup chopped green onion

1. Preheat oven to 350° F.

2. Wrap potatoes individually in aluminum foil. Bake for 1 hour.

3. While potatoes are baking, combine barbecue sauce and wine in a mixing bowl. Toss chicken thoroughly with ⅓ of sauce. Reserve remaining sauce. Coat four 12-inch skewers with a low-calorie cooking spray. Thread chicken onto skewers, alternating with green or red pepper. When potatoes are done, remove from oven, and heat broiler.

4. Place skewers on broiler rack and broil 2–3 inches away from heat source for 2–3 minutes on each side. Meanwhile, split potatoes almost in half and fluff with a fork, being careful not to tear skin. Remove chicken and peppers from skewers and place on potatoes. Spoon 1 teaspoon barbecue sauce on top, then sprinkle with grated cheese and green onion. Place in warm oven until cheese melts, about 3–4 minutes.

Do Not Freeze

SWEET CRADLES OF INDIA

Serves 4   **Approximately 7.1 g fat, 200 mg sodium per serving**

Curried chicken in sweetly spiced acorn squash.

2 acorn squash (about 1 pound each), halved and seeded
¼ cup dark brown sugar, not packed
1 teaspoon apple pie spice
Low-calorie cooking spray
¾ pound chicken breast meat, cut into bite-sized pieces
¼ teaspoon salt (if desired)
¼ teaspoon freshly ground black pepper
1 cup chopped yellow onion
¾ cup apple juice
3 tablespoons chopped dates
¼ cup pecans, toasted under broiler
2 teaspoons curry powder
½ teaspoon cinnamon
¼ teaspoon orange zest
⅛ teaspoon ground cloves
⅛ teaspoon ground ginger
⅛ teaspoon ground nutmeg

1. Preheat oven to 350° F.
2. Sprinkle each squash half with 1 tablespoon brown sugar and ¼ teaspoon apple pie spice. Place on foil-lined oven rack and bake for 40 minutes.
3. While squash is baking, coat a nonstick skillet with a low-calorie cooking spray. Add chicken, salt, and black pepper, and brown over medium-high heat for 5–6 minutes. Drain and discard excess grease. Place chicken on paper towels to remove additional grease.
4. Add onion to skillet and sauté 3–4 minutes over medium-high heat. Reduce heat to medium and add chicken, apple juice, dates, pecans, curry powder, cinnamon, orange zest, cloves, ginger, and nutmeg. Simmer 2 minutes. Spoon mixture into squash halves. Cover and bake for 20–25 minutes, or until squash is tender.

Do Not Freeze

❋ ❋

HOT AND SPICY SESAME CHICKEN

Serves 4   **Approximately 9.3 g fat, 431 mg sodium per serving**

Spicy-sweet, peanut-flavored chicken with broccoli and sesame seeds.

1½ cups water
3 cups fresh broccoli flowerets
Low-calorie cooking spray
1 teaspoon sesame oil
1 pound chicken breast meat, cut
  into bite-sized pieces
1 8-ounce can sliced water
  chestnuts, well drained
2 green onions, diagonally sliced
  in 1-inch strips
1½ tablespoons cornstarch
1 tablespoon plus 2 teaspoons all-
  natural peanut butter
2 tablespoons low-sodium soy
  sauce
¼–½ teaspoon red pepper flakes to
  taste
¼ teaspoon freshly grated ginger
  root
⅛ teaspoon curry powder
3 tablespoons dark brown sugar,
  packed
2 tablespoons sesame seeds,
  toasted under broiler

1. In a 10-inch nonstick skillet, bring ½ cup water to a boil. Add broccoli, reduce heat, cover tightly, and simmer 4 minutes until tender but still crisp. Drain well. Place broccoli on a serving plate, cover with aluminum foil, and keep warm. Wipe skillet dry with a paper towel.

2. Coat skillet with a low-calorie cooking spray. Add sesame oil to skillet and heat. Add chicken and cook over high heat, stirring constantly, for 3 minutes. Add water chestnuts and green onions.

3. In a small mixing bowl, combine cornstarch, the remaining 1 cup water, peanut butter, soy sauce, red pepper flakes, ginger root, curry powder, and brown sugar. Mix well and add to skillet with chicken mixture. Bring to a boil, stirring constantly. Cook 2 minutes or until thickened. Spoon onto serving platter next to broccoli. Sprinkle all with toasted sesame seeds and serve immediately.

Do Not Freeze

❋ ❋

HONEY-GLAZED ORIENTAL CHICKEN AND SPINACH SALAD

Serves 4

Approximately 9.0 g fat, 411 mg sodium per serving

1 tablespoon sesame oil
2 tablespoons low-sodium soy sauce
1 tablespoon dark brown sugar, packed
1 tablespoon honey
½ teaspoon ground ginger
⅛ teaspoon curry powder
2 garlic cloves, minced
¼–½ teaspoon red pepper flakes
⅛ teaspoon freshly ground black pepper
1½ teaspoons fresh lime juice
1 pound chicken breast meat, cut into ½-inch pieces
4 cups fresh spinach leaves
2 cups fresh watercress leaves
½ cup matchstick-sized pieces fresh carrot
¼ cup freshly chopped red onion
1 orange, halved and thinly sliced
Low-calorie cooking spray
¼ cup water
1 tablespoon sesame seeds, toasted under broiler

1. In a 1-gallon freezer bag, combine sesame oil, soy sauce, sugar, honey, ginger, curry powder, garlic, red pepper flakes, black pepper, and lime juice. Mix thoroughly and add chicken. Seal bag, releasing any excess air. Shake to coat chicken thoroughly. Marinate in refrigerator for 30 minutes.

2. While chicken is marinating, place 1 cup spinach and ½ cup watercress on each dinner plate. Top greens with 2 tablespoons carrot and 1 tablespoon onion. Arrange ¼ of the orange slices on the side of each plate.

3. Coat a 10-inch nonstick skillet with a low-calorie cooking spray. Place skillet over high heat for 1 minute. Remove chicken from marinade, reserving marinade, and stir-fry in hot skillet 2–3 minutes, or until chicken is no longer pink in the center. Add water, and scrape sides and bottom of skillet. Add marinade. Reduce heat and simmer about 2 minutes, or until chicken is richly glazed.

4. Place ¼ of chicken mixture on top of each plate. Sprinkle sesame seeds over all. Serve immediately.

Do Not Freeze

CHINESE CHICKEN STIR-FRY

Serves 4

Approximately 9.6 g fat, 460 mg sodium per serving

Low-calorie cooking spray
2 tablespoons sesame oil
6 cups shredded bok choy or cabbage
1 cup sliced yellow onion
⅛ teaspoon black pepper
1 tablespoon plus 1½ teaspoons low-sodium soy sauce
½ teaspoon freshly grated ginger root
½ teaspoon minced garlic
½ pound chicken breast meat, cut into thin strips
1½ cups broccoli flowerets
1 red bell pepper, thinly sliced
¼ cup water
½ 6-ounce package frozen pea pods
½ cup water chestnuts, well drained
¼–½ teaspoon red pepper flakes
2 tablespoons hoisin sauce
½ teaspoon sugar
1 cup chow mein noodles

1. Coat a large skillet or wok with a low-calorie cooking spray. Heat 1 tablespoon of the sesame oil over high heat. Add bok choy, onion, and black pepper. Stir-fry 3–4 minutes, or until vegetables are tender but still crisp. Toss with 1 tablespoon plus 1½ teaspoons of the soy sauce. Spoon onto a serving platter and keep warm.

2. To skillet or wok, add 1 teaspoon sesame oil with ginger root and garlic. Sauté 1 minute. Add chicken and cook 3 minutes longer, or until done. Remove chicken mixture and set aside.

3. Heat remaining 2 teaspoons oil for 1 minute. Add broccoli and sweet red pepper, and cook for 2–3 minutes. Add water, cover tightly, and cook 3–4 minutes longer. Add pea pods, water chestnuts, red pepper flakes, hoisin sauce, sugar, and chicken. Cook 2 minutes longer.

4. Spoon mixture over cabbage and sprinkle with remaining 1 tablespoon soy sauce and chow mein noodles. Serve immediately.

Do Not Freeze

CITRUS-WALNUT CHICKEN WITH CURRANTS

Serves 4

Approximately 5.9 g fat, 149 mg sodium per serving

2 cups hot cooked rice (no margarine or salt added during cooking)

¼ cup finely chopped green bell pepper

⅛ teaspoon turmeric

⅛ teaspoon curry powder

¼ cup chopped dried currants or dates

2 tablespoons plus 1 teaspoon orange marmalade

2 teaspoons low-sodium soy sauce

1½ teaspoons fresh lemon juice

½ teaspoon lemon zest

3 tablespoons walnuts, toasted under broiler

Low-calorie cooking spray

1 medium yellow onion, thinly sliced

¾ pound boneless chicken breast meat, cut into bite-sized pieces

1. Place rice, green pepper, turmeric, and curry powder in a bowl. Toss together well and place on serving platter. Cover with aluminum foil and place in warm oven.

2. In small mixing bowl, combine currants, marmalade, soy sauce, lemon juice, and lemon zest and set aside.

3. Coat a 10-inch nonstick skillet with a low-calorie cooking spray. Heat 1 minute over medium-high heat and add onion. Cook 3–4 minutes or until browned. Make a well in center of rice and place onions in center of well. Cover and keep warm.

4. Coat the skillet again with a low-calorie cooking spray. Increase heat to high. Heat 1 minute and add chicken. Cook 2–3 minutes, stirring constantly, until chicken is no longer pink in center. Remove chicken and place on top of onions. Add water to skillet and scrape sides and bottom of skillet. Reduce heat to medium-high, add currant-marmalade mixture, stir in walnuts, and cook 1 minute. Spoon over all and serve immediately.

Do Not Freeze

4
❧ TURKEY ❧

Peppered Turkey and Vegetable Stew
Cracked-Pepper Turkey with Mushrooms
Spaghetti with Meatballs
Best-Ever Chili
Chili-and-Cheese Omelettes
Smoky Turkey Ham and Mixed Vegetables in Cheese
Turkey Ham and Potato Latkes
Scalloped "Ham" and Potatoes
Eggplant Louise
Jalapeño "Ham" and Corn
Crustless Turkey Ham and Vegetable Quiche
"Ham"-Tossed Rice with Brown-Sugared Pineapple
Monterey "Ham" with Jalapeños
Ratatouille with Turkey Sausage in French Bread Shells
Sweet Turkey Sausage in Cream Sauce with Pasta
Cheesy Eggplant and Sausage Casserole
Mexican Stuffed Peppers
Autumn Sausage and Rice Casserole
Sausage and Cheddar Crustless Tart

PEPPERED TURKEY AND VEGETABLE STEW

Serves 4

Approximately 4.0 g fat, 491 mg sodium per serving

2 tablespoons flour
Low-calorie cooking spray
1 pound turkey tenderloin, cut
 into bite-sized pieces
10 small new potatoes (about 1
 ounce each), halved
4 medium carrots, peeled and cut
 into 3-inch pieces
1 medium yellow onion, cut into
 eighths
2 cups 2-inch-long pieces fresh
 green beans
1 cup 1-inch-long pieces celery
4 garlic cloves, minced
1¼ cups water
1 teaspoon beef bouillon granules
¾ cup dry red wine
½ cup thin strips green bell pepper
3 tablespoons chopped fresh
 parsley
1 teaspoon dried basil leaves
½ teaspoon freshly ground black
 pepper
¼ teaspoon salt (if desired)

1. Preheat oven to 350° F.
2. In a dry dutch oven, preferably cast-iron, heat flour over medium heat, stirring until the color changes from white to off-white, about 10–13 minutes. Remove pot from heat and set flour aside.
3. Coat dutch oven with a low-calorie cooking spray. Heat 1 minute over medium-high heat. Add turkey, potatoes, carrots, onion, green beans, celery, and garlic. Sauté, stirring frequently, about 8–10 minutes. Sprinkle in flour. Add water, beef bouillon granules, wine, green pepper, parsley, basil, and black pepper.
4. Cover tightly and bake for 45–50 minutes, or until vegetables are tender. Stir in salt and serve.

Variation: If a thicker sauce is desired, complete step 3 by mixing 1 tablespoon cornstarch with 3 tablespoons cold water. Stir into stew and cook 3–4 minutes longer, or until thickened.

MAKE-AHEAD MEAL DIRECTIONS

To Freeze: Complete steps 1–3 of the recipe, omitting potatoes. (Note: Do not continue to step 4.) Cover tightly and bake for 45–50 minutes, or until vegetables are tender. Add uncooked potatoes and let stew cool completely.

Place in two 1-gallon freezer bags. Seal each bag tightly, allowing no excess air to remain, and freeze. This can be kept frozen for up to 1 month.

To Prepare for Serving: Let mixture thaw completely. Pour into a dutch oven and cover tightly. Heat thoroughly over moderate heat for about 40 minutes, or until potatoes are tender, stirring occasionally. Stir in salt and serve.

❖ ⋅ ❖

CRACKED-PEPPER TURKEY WITH MUSHROOMS

Serves 4

Approximately 5.4 g fat, 468 mg sodium per serving

Low-calorie cooking spray
½ pound mushrooms, sliced
¾ pound turkey cutlets, cut into bite-sized pieces
½ teaspoon low-sodium Worcestershire sauce
2 garlic cloves, minced
1 teaspoon butter
2 tablespoons finely chopped green onion
½ cup dry white wine
½ cup evaporated skim milk
1 cup skim milk
¼ teaspoon nutmeg
¾ teaspoon beef bouillon granules
¼ teaspoon salt (if desired)
1 tablespoon cornstarch
2 tablespoons water
1 teaspoon cracked black pepper
3 cups hot cooked fettuccine (no salt added during cooking)
1 tablespoon plus 1 teaspoon freshly grated Parmesan cheese

1. Coat a 10-inch nonstick skillet with a low-calorie cooking spray. Heat skillet over high heat for 1 minute. Add mushrooms and sauté, stirring frequently, for 2–3 minutes. Remove from skillet and set aside on a serving platter.

2. In the same skillet, cook turkey, Worcestershire sauce, and garlic over medium-high heat, stirring constantly, until the turkey turns a rich brown, about 3 minutes. With a slotted spoon, remove turkey from skillet and add to mushrooms. Add butter to any pan drippings. Melt butter and add 1 tablespoon green onion. Sauté 20 seconds. Add wine and boil 4 minutes, or until liquid has almost evaporated. Reduce heat to medium and add evaporated milk, skim milk, nutmeg, and beef bouillon granules. Simmer 7 minutes, stirring frequently. Add salt, turkey, and mushrooms with any accumulated liquid to sauce in skillet. Blend thoroughly.

3. In a small glass, combine cornstarch and water, and blend well. Stir into meat mixture and add cracked pepper. Cook, stirring, for 2–3 minutes, or until thickened.

4. Place fettuccine on a serving platter and spoon sauce on top. Sprinkle with remaining 1 tablespoon minced green onion and Parmesan cheese.

MAKE-AHEAD MEAL DIRECTIONS

To Freeze: Complete steps 1–2 of the recipe. (Note: Do not continue to step 3.) Let turkey mixture cool completely. Place in a 1-gallon freezer bag. Seal bag tightly, allowing no excess air to remain, and freeze. This can be kept frozen for up to 1 month.

To Prepare for Serving: Let mixture thaw completely. Pour into a medium saucepan and heat thoroughly over moderate heat—*do not boil*. Complete steps 3–4 of the recipe.

SPAGHETTI WITH MEATBALLS

Serves 4

Approximately 9.5 g fat, 445 mg sodium per serving

1½ cups frozen chopped spinach, thawed
10 ounces ground turkey
½ slice reduced-calorie bread, toasted and grated
1 egg white
⅓ cup finely chopped green onion
½ teaspoon dried basil leaves
2 garlic cloves, minced
¼ teaspoon freshly ground black pepper
¼ teaspoon fennel seeds
¼ teaspoon nutmeg
⅛ teaspoon allspice
¼ teaspoon dried sage leaves
¼ teaspoon salt (if desired)
Low-calorie cooking spray
1 teaspoon extra-virgin olive oil
1 cup thinly sliced fresh mushrooms
½ cup finely chopped yellow onion
¼ cup finely chopped green bell pepper
1 cup (half of 1 16-ounce can) canned chopped tomatoes, undrained
⅓ cup tomato paste
2 tablespoons dry red wine
½ teaspoon dried oregano leaves
½ teaspoon sugar
3 cups hot cooked spaghetti (no salt added during cooking)
2 tablespoons freshly grated Romano cheese
¼ cup chopped fresh parsley

1. Drain spinach and squeeze out excess liquid. In a mixing bowl, combine spinach with ground turkey, bread crumbs, egg white, green onion, basil, garlic, black pepper, fennel, nutmeg, allspice, sage, and salt. Mix well and shape into 40 meatballs.

2. Coat a 10-inch nonstick skillet with a low-calorie cooking spray. Add oil and heat over medium-high heat. Add meatballs and cook until browned, about 6 minutes. Drain and discard excess grease. Place meatballs on paper towels to remove additional grease. Wipe skillet dry with a paper towel.

3. In same skillet, sauté mushrooms, onion, and green pepper over medium-high heat until browned, about 2–3 minutes. Add tomatoes, tomato paste, wine, oregano, and sugar. Stir well. Add meatballs and bring to a boil. Reduce heat, cover tightly, and simmer 30 minutes.

4. Place spaghetti on a serving platter. Top with meatballs and sauce, cheese, and parsley.

MAKE-AHEAD MEAL DIRECTIONS

To Freeze: Complete steps 1–3 of the recipe. (Note: Do not continue to step 4.) Place sauce and meatballs in an 8-inch square foil pan. Let cool completely, wrap tightly with freezer foil, and freeze. This can be kept frozen for up to 1 month.

To Prepare for Serving: Let mixture thaw completely. Preheat oven to 350° F. Place wrapped container in oven and bake for 30–40 minutes, or until heated thoroughly. Place spaghetti on a serving platter. Top with meatballs and sauce, cheese, and parsley.

BEST-EVER CHILI

Serves 4   **Approximately 9.9 g fat, 449 mg sodium per serving**

Chili fortified with a hint of red wine, topped with a light sour cream, and ringed with finely chopped green onion.

Low-calorie cooking spray
3 garlic cloves, minced
2 cups chopped yellow onion
1 cup chopped celery
⅔ pound ground turkey
1 28-ounce can chopped tomatoes, undrained
2 green bell peppers, chopped
2 jalapeño peppers, finely chopped
3 tablespoons dry red wine
¼ cup chopped fresh parsley
2 tablespoons chili powder
2 teaspoons sugar
1 teaspoon dried oregano leaves
½ teaspoon cumin
¼ teaspoon ground red pepper
⅛ teaspoon freshly ground black pepper
⅛ teaspoon salt (if desired)
Dash ground cloves
1 cup canned kidney beans, drained and rinsed
2 tablespoons plus 2 teaspoons light sour cream
¼ cup finely chopped green onion

1. Coat a dutch oven, preferably cast-iron, with a low-calorie cooking spray. Over medium-high heat, sauté garlic 1 minute. Add onion and celery, and sauté about 4–5 minutes, or until tender but still crisp. Add ground turkey and brown, about 5 minutes.

2. Stir in tomatoes and liquid, bell peppers, jalapeño peppers, wine, parsley, chili powder, sugar, oregano, cumin, red pepper, black pepper, salt, and cloves. Stir well. Bring to a boil, reduce heat, and simmer, uncovered, for 30 minutes, stirring occasionally. Stir in beans and simmer 5 minutes longer.

3. Top each serving with 2 teaspoons sour cream in center of chili. Sprinkle 1 tablespoon chopped green onion in a ring around sour cream.

MAKE-AHEAD MEAL DIRECTIONS

To Freeze: Complete steps 1–2 of the recipe. (Note: Do not continue to step 3.) Let chili cool completely. Place in two 1-gallon freezer bags. Seal each bag tightly, allowing no excess air to remain, and freeze. This can be kept frozen for up to 1 month.

To Prepare for Serving: Let chili thaw completely. Pour into a dutch oven and cover. Heat thoroughly over medium heat, stirring occasionally. Garnish and serve as directed in step 3 of the recipe.

CHILI-AND-CHEESE OMELETTES

Serves 4

Approximately 6.7 fat, 477 mg sodium per serving

Low-calorie cooking spray
½ pound ground turkey
¼ cup chopped yellow onion
1 garlic clove, minced
1 teaspoon chili powder
¾ teaspoon cumin
½ teaspoon dried oregano leaves
⅛ teaspoon red pepper flakes
3 tablespoons water
½ cup chopped green bell pepper
¼ cup prepared hot salsa
16 large egg whites
½ cup skim milk
½ cup (2 ounces) shredded
  mozzarella cheese
¼ cup finely chopped red onion

1. Coat a 10-inch nonstick skillet with a low-calorie cooking spray. Over medium-high heat, add ground turkey, onion, and garlic. Brown, stirring frequently, about 4 minutes. Drain and discard excess grease. Place turkey mixture on paper towels to remove additional grease.

2. Return turkey mixture to skillet and add chili powder, cumin, oregano, and red pepper flakes. Reduce heat and simmer 2 minutes. Add water, green pepper, and salsa. Stir well. Transfer mixture to a plate and set aside. Using a paper towel, wipe skillet dry.

3. Recoat skillet with low-calorie cooking spray. In a separate bowl, whisk together 4 egg whites with 2 tablespoons milk. Place skillet over medium heat and add egg mixture. Lift the edges of eggs with a spatula as they cook, letting the uncooked part run underneath until the omelette is set. Spoon ½ cup meat filling over half of the omelette. Fold omelette over and top with 2 tablespoons cheese. Place on a plate and keep warm. Repeat this procedure for the remaining 3 omelettes. Just before serving, sprinkle each with 1 tablespoon red onion.

MAKE-AHEAD MEAL DIRECTIONS

To Freeze: Complete steps 1–2 of the recipe. (Note: Do not continue to step 3.) Let turkey mixture cool completely. Place in a 1-quart freezer bag. Seal bag tightly, allowing no excess air to remain, and freeze. This can be kept frozen for up to 1 month.

To Prepare for Serving: Let mixture thaw completely. Pour into a 10-inch nonstick skillet. Heat thoroughly over moderate heat, stirring frequently. Transfer to a plate and set aside. Wipe skillet dry with a paper towel. Prepare omelettes as directed in step 3 of the recipe.

SMOKY TURKEY HAM AND MIXED VEGETABLES IN CHEESE

Serves 4

Approximately 6.8 g fat, 488 mg sodium per serving

Low-calorie cooking spray
¼ pound turkey ham, thinly sliced, then chopped
1 cup water
2 10-ounce packages frozen mixed vegetables
¾ cup evaporated skim milk
1½ tablespoons flour
½ cup plus 1½ tablespoons (2½ ounces) grated low-sodium, reduced-fat sharp cheddar cheese
⅛ teaspoon black pepper
39 small cheese crackers, crushed (about ⅔ cup)

1. Preheat oven to 350° F.
2. Coat a 10-inch ovenproof nonstick skillet with a low-calorie cooking spray. Over medium heat, add turkey ham and sauté 3 minutes. Remove from skillet and set aside.
3. Bring water to a boil in skillet over high heat. Add vegetables. Return to a boil, reduce heat, cover tightly, and simmer 8 minutes. Drain well, remove from skillet, and set aside with turkey ham.
4. Place skillet over medium heat and add milk. Whisk in flour. Stirring with a flat spatula, cook until thickened, 1–2 minutes. Remove from heat and add cheese and black pepper. Stir until melted. (Sauce will have lumps at this point.) Stir in drained vegetables and turkey ham, and blend well.
5. Top with cracker crumbs. Bake for 15–18 minutes, or until heated thoroughly.

MAKE-AHEAD MEAL DIRECTIONS

To Freeze: Complete steps 2–4 of the recipe. (Note: Do not continue to step 5.) Let mixture cool completely. Wrap skillet tightly with freezer foil, and freeze. This can be kept frozen for up to 1 month.

To Prepare for Serving: Let mixture thaw completely. Preheat oven to 350° F. Unwrap skillet and stir casserole. Top with cracker crumbs and bake uncovered for 30 minutes, or until heated thoroughly.

TURKEY HAM AND POTATO LATKES

Serves 4

Approximately 8.6 g fat, 495 mg sodium per serving

6 ounces turkey ham, thinly sliced, then chopped (about 1½ cups)
14 ounces peeled potatoes, shredded
¾ cup shredded yellow onion
3 egg whites
¼ cup flour
1 tablespoon chopped fresh parsley
¼ teaspoon paprika
¼ teaspoon freshly ground black pepper
Low-calorie cooking spray
1 tablespoon vegetable oil
1 tablespoon butter or margarine

1. In a mixing bowl, combine turkey ham, potatoes, onion, egg whites, flour, parsley, paprika, and black pepper. Mix well. Shape into 8 patties, about ¼ inch thick. (This mixture will be *very* moist.)

2. Coat a 10-inch nonstick skillet with a low-calorie cooking spray. Over medium-high heat, add 1½ teaspoons oil and 1½ teaspoons butter or margarine. Heat 1 minute. Add 4 of the patties. Cook 3–4 minutes on each side.

3. Remove from skillet and set aside in a warm oven. Repeat process with remaining oil, butter, and patties.

MAKE-AHEAD MEAL DIRECTIONS

To Freeze: Complete steps 1–3 of the recipe. Let patties cool completely. Place in two 1-gallon freezer bags in a single layer. Seal bags tightly, allowing no excess air to remain, and freeze. This can be kept frozen for up to 1 month.

To Prepare for Serving: Let patties thaw completely. Preheat oven to 475° F. Place on ungreased cookie sheets and bake for 15 minutes.

SCALLOPED "HAM" AND POTATOES

Serves 4

Approximately 4.9 g fat, 487 mg sodium per serving

Low-calorie cooking spray
1¼ pounds peeled potatoes, thinly
  sliced
5 ounces turkey ham, thinly
  sliced, then cut in julienne
  strips
3 tablespoons flour
3 tablespoons low-calorie
  margarine
⅛ teaspoon freshly ground black
  pepper
1¾ cups evaporated skim milk

1. Preheat oven to 350° F.

2. Coat an 8-inch square baking dish with a low-calorie cooking spray. Place ¼ of the potatoes on bottom of dish. Top with ¼ of the turkey ham, flour, and margarine. Repeat layers 3 more times. Sprinkle with black pepper. Pour milk over all.

3. Cover and bake 30 minutes. Uncover and bake 1 hour, or until potatoes are tender. Let stand 5–8 minutes before serving.

MAKE-AHEAD MEAL DIRECTIONS

To Freeze: Complete steps 2–3 of the recipe, using an 8-inch square foil pan in place of baking dish. Let mixture cool completely, wrap tightly with freezer foil, and freeze. This can be kept frozen for up to 1 month.

To Prepare for Serving: Let mixture thaw completely. Preheat oven to 350° F. Place wrapped container in oven and bake for 35–40 minutes, or until heated thoroughly. Let stand 5–8 minutes before serving.

❧ ❧

EGGPLANT LOUISE

Serves 4

Approximately 9.5 g fat, 365 mg sodium per serving

3 slices "lower-salt" bacon
6 garlic cloves, minced
2½ cups chopped yellow onion
1½ cups chopped red bell pepper
8 cups (about 2 pounds) peeled and diced eggplant
¾ cup dry white wine
½ teaspoon sugar
¾ teaspoon dried thyme leaves
⅜ teaspoon freshly ground black pepper
½ teaspoon low-sodium Worcestershire sauce
½ teaspoon Cajun seasoning
1½ ounces turkey ham, thinly sliced and chopped
½ cup (2 ounces) grated reduced-fat Swiss cheese
¼ cup plus 2 tablespoons (1½ ounces) grated low-sodium, reduced-fat sharp cheddar cheese

1. Preheat oven to 350° F.

2. In a dutch oven, preferably cast-iron, fry bacon over medium-high heat until crisp. Remove bacon and drain on a paper towel. Discard all but 2 tablespoons of the pan drippings. Crumble bacon and set aside.

3. Add garlic to drippings and sauté 1 minute over medium-high heat. Add onion and sweet red pepper, and brown about 5 minutes. Add eggplant, wine, sugar, thyme, black pepper, and bacon. Cook uncovered for 6 minutes, stirring occasionally. Reduce heat, cover tightly, and simmer 35 minutes. Add Worcestershire sauce, Cajun seasoning, and turkey ham. Stir well.

4. Bake uncovered for 15 minutes. Top with Swiss and cheddar cheeses and bake 5–6 minutes longer, or until cheese melts. Serve immediately.

Variation: Omit 1 tablespoon bacon grease and the turkey ham, substituting 1 cup cooked shrimp.

MAKE-AHEAD MEAL DIRECTIONS

To Freeze: Complete steps 2–3 of the recipe. (Note: Do not continue to step 4.) Place mixture in an 8-inch square foil pan. Let cool completely, wrap tightly with freezer foil, and freeze. This can be kept frozen for up to 1 month (up to 2 weeks if shrimp is substituted for turkey ham.)

To Prepare for Serving: Let mixture thaw completely. Preheat oven to 325° F. Place wrapped container in oven and bake for 40 minutes. Unwrap, top with Swiss and cheddar cheeses, and bake 5–10 minutes longer, or until heated thoroughly. Sprinkle with Parmesan cheese and serve immediately.

JALAPEÑO "HAM" AND CORN

Serves 4   Approximately 9.4 g fat, 459 mg sodium per serving

A hearty cornmeal-based dish with smoked turkey ham, corn, and jalapeño peppers, served with baked tomatoes.

Low-calorie cooking spray
3½ ounces turkey ham, thinly
   sliced, then chopped (about 1
   cup)
⅔ cup thin strips green bell
   pepper
½ cup cornmeal
1 cup nonfat buttermilk
1 cup frozen corn kernels
2 jalapeño peppers, finely
   chopped
2 egg whites
1 tablespoon vegetable oil
½ teaspoon baking powder
¼ teaspoon garlic powder
¾ cup (3 ounces) shredded
   reduced-fat, low-sodium sharp
   cheddar cheese
4 teaspoons Dijon mustard
2 medium tomatoes, halved
4 teaspoons chopped fresh parsley
Dash lemon pepper, if desired

1. Preheat oven to 350° F.
2. Coat a 10-inch ovenproof nonstick skillet with a low-calorie cooking spray. Over medium-high heat, add turkey ham and green pepper. Sauté 4–5 minutes. Remove from heat. Stir in cornmeal, buttermilk, corn, jalapeño peppers, egg whites, oil, baking powder, garlic powder, and ½ cup cheddar cheese. Blend well.
3. Bake uncovered for 10 minutes. While casserole is baking, spread 1 teaspoon mustard over each tomato half and sprinkle each with 1 teaspoon parsley. After the 10 minutes have passed, place tomatoes on a foil-lined oven rack and bake with casserole 25 minutes longer. Remove from oven.
4. Sprinkle remaining ¼ cup cheese on casserole. Let stand 5 minutes and serve with tomato halves. Sprinkle tomatoes with lemon pepper.

MAKE-AHEAD MEAL DIRECTIONS

To Freeze: Complete step 2 of the recipe, omitting baking powder. (Note: Do not continue to step 3.) Wrap skillet tightly with freezer foil, and freeze. This can be kept frozen for up to 1 month.

To Prepare for Serving: Let mixture thaw completely. Preheat oven to 350° F. Unwrap skillet, add baking powder, and blend well. Bake casserole and prepare tomatoes as directed in steps 3–4 of the recipe.

CRUSTLESS TURKEY HAM AND VEGETABLE QUICHE

Serves 4

Approximately 7.5 g fat, 392 mg sodium

1 teaspoon vegetable oil
1 green bell pepper, chopped
1 cup sliced yellow onion
3½ ounces turkey ham, thinly sliced, then chopped (about 1 cup)
⅛ teaspoon garlic powder
Low-calorie cooking spray
4 large eggs
⅓ cup evaporated skim milk
1 tablespoon Dijon mustard
⅛ teaspoon cayenne pepper
Freshly ground black pepper to taste

1. Preheat oven to 350° F.
2. In a 10-inch nonstick skillet, heat oil over medium-high heat for 1 minute. Add green pepper, onion, turkey ham, and garlic powder. Sauté 8 minutes. Remove from heat and set aside.
3. Coat a 9-inch pie pan with a low-calorie cooking spray. Add eggs, milk, mustard, cayenne, and black pepper. Blend well. Stir in sautéed ham and vegetables. Mix thoroughly.
4. Bake for 25 minutes, or until quiche has set. Let stand 5 minutes before serving.

MAKE-AHEAD MEAL DIRECTIONS

To Freeze: Complete steps 1–4 of the recipe. Let quiche cool completely. Wrap tightly with freezer foil and freeze. This can be kept frozen for up to 2 weeks.

To Prepare for Serving: Let quiche thaw completely. Preheat oven to 350° F. Unwrap quiche and bake for 20 minutes. Let stand 5 minutes before serving.

❧ ❧

"HAM"-TOSSED RICE WITH BROWN-SUGARED PINEAPPLE

Serves 4

Approximately 1.7 g fat, 290 mg sodium per serving

2 8-ounce cans pineapple tidbits
   in juice, undrained
2 tablespoons dark brown sugar,
   packed
¼ teaspoon cinnamon
⅛ teaspoon ground cloves
1 tablespoon cornstarch
3½ cups hot cooked rice (no
   margarine or salt added during
   cooking)
¼ pound turkey ham, thinly
   sliced, then chopped (1 cup)
¼ cup slivered green bell pepper (if
   desired)

1. Preheat broiler.
2. In a 10-inch ovenproof nonstick skillet, combine pineapple, brown sugar, cinnamon, cloves, and cornstarch. Blend well. Place over high heat, bring to a boil, and cook 2 minutes, or until thickened. Remove from heat. Spoon mixture into a small mixing bowl and set aside.
3. In the same skillet, layer rice, turkey ham, and bell pepper, if desired. Top with pineapple sauce. Broil at least 5 inches from heat source for 3–4 minutes, or until bubbly.

Do Not Freeze

MONTEREY "HAM" WITH JALAPEÑOS

Serves 4

Approximately 8.7 g fat, 472 mg sodium per serving

Turkey ham, sweet red peppers, and jalapeños baked in a creamy white cheese sauce.

1 cup skim milk
1 tablespoon flour
¾ cup shredded Monterey Jack
   cheese with jalapeño peppers
2 jalapeño peppers, minced
2 green onions, chopped
¼ cup chopped red bell pepper
¼ pound turkey ham, chopped
   (about 1 cup)
⅛ teaspoon freshly ground black
   pepper
4 cups hot cooked macaroni
   (about 8 ounces dry) (no salt
   added during cooking)
Fresh parsley

1. Place a nonstick dutch oven over medium heat. Add milk, whisk in flour, and cook 5–7 minutes, stirring frequently with a flat spatula, until thickened. Stir in cheese, jalapeño peppers, green onions, sweet red pepper, turkey ham, and black pepper. Remove from heat.

2. Add cooked macaroni and blend thoroughly. Top with fresh parsley.

Do Not Freeze

RATATOUILLE WITH TURKEY SAUSAGE IN FRENCH BREAD SHELLS

Serves 4

Approximately 8.0 g fat, 495 mg sodium per serving

Italian vegetables simmered with sausage, served in hollowed French rolls, and topped with mozzarella.

Low-calorie cooking spray
5 ounces turkey kielbasa links, cut into ⅛-inch slices
½ cup chopped yellow onion
1 cup quartered fresh mushrooms
2 garlic cloves, minced
2 cups peeled and diced eggplant
2 cups thinly sliced zucchini
1 16-ounce can unsalted chopped tomatoes, drained
1 green bell pepper, sliced thin
¼ teaspoon red pepper flakes
¼ cup chopped fresh parsley
¼ teaspoon sugar
½ teaspoon dried oregano leaves
½ teaspoon dried basil leaves
⅛ teaspoon freshly ground black pepper
4 individual French bread rolls (1½ ounces each)
½ cup (2 ounces) shredded mozzarella cheese
2 teaspoons grated Parmesan cheese

1. Preheat oven to 350° F.

2. Coat a 10-inch nonstick skillet with a low-calorie cooking spray. Over medium-high heat, brown sausage slices for about 2–3 minutes. Remove from skillet.

3. To any remaining pan drippings, add onion, mushrooms, and garlic, and sauté for 4 minutes. Add eggplant, zucchini, tomatoes, green pepper, red pepper flakes, parsley, sugar, oregano, basil, and black pepper. Stir well. Bring to a boil, cover tightly, reduce heat, and simmer 20 minutes, or until eggplant is tender. Stir in sausage slices.

4. Split rolls in half lengthwise. Remove and discard soft bread in center, leaving the outer shell intact. Bake bread shells for 3 minutes.

5. Remove from oven and fill with vegetable mixture. Top each half with 2 tablespoons mozzarella. Bake 5 minutes longer, or until cheese melts. Sprinkle with Parmesan cheese and serve.

MAKE-AHEAD MEAL DIRECTIONS

To Freeze: Complete steps 2–3 of the recipe. (Note: Do not continue to step 4.) Let mixture cool completely. Place in a 1-gallon freezer bag. Seal bag tightly, allowing no excess air to remain, and freeze. (Rolls may be frozen separately, if desired, for up to 2 weeks.) This can be kept frozen for up to 1 month.

To Prepare for Serving: Let mixture (and rolls, if frozen) thaw completely. Preheat oven to 350° F. Pour mixture into a large saucepan and heat thoroughly over moderate heat, stirring frequently. Prepare bread shells and bake as directed in steps 4–5 of the recipe.

❋ ❋

SWEET TURKEY SAUSAGE IN CREAM SAUCE WITH PASTA

Serves 4   **Approximately 9.1 g fat, 410 mg sodium per serving**

Italian sausage in a rich cream sauce, tossed with green beans and served over fusilli.

Low-calorie cooking spray
½ pound sweet Italian turkey
  sausage
2 cups quartered fresh mushrooms
2 garlic cloves, minced
¼ cup chopped yellow onion
1 teaspoon low-sodium
  Worcestershire sauce
½ cup evaporated skim milk
1 teaspoon dried oregano leaves
⅛ teaspoon freshly ground black
  pepper
1 8-ounce can no-salt French-style
  green beans, well drained
3 cups hot cooked fusilli
  (corkscrew pasta) (about 6
  ounces dry) (no salt added
  during cooking)
2 tablespoons chopped fresh
  parsley
3 tablespoons grated Parmesan
  cheese

1. Coat a 10-inch nonstick skillet with a low-calorie cooking spray. Over medium-high heat, brown sausage, stirring frequently, about 5 minutes. Drain and discard excess grease. Place sausage on paper towels to remove additional grease. Wipe skillet dry with a paper towel.

2. In the same skillet, sauté mushrooms, garlic, and onion over medium-high heat until lightly browned, about 3–4 minutes. Add Worcestershire sauce, evaporated milk, oregano, and black pepper. Reduce heat and simmer uncovered for 3–4 minutes, or until sauce is slightly thickened.

3. Add sausage and blend well. Add well-drained beans and stir. Heat 2–3 minutes, uncovered.

4. Place hot fusilli on serving platter. Sprinkle with parsley and spoon meat sauce over pasta. Top with Parmesan cheese and serve immediately.

MAKE-AHEAD MEAL DIRECTIONS

To Freeze: Complete steps 1–2 of the recipe. (Note: Do not continue to step 3.) Add sausage and blend well. Let mixture cool completely. Place in a 1-quart freezer bag. Seal bag tightly, allowing no excess air to remain, and freeze. This can be kept frozen for up to 1 month.

To Prepare for Serving: Let sausage mixture thaw completely. Pour mixture into a medium saucepan and heat thoroughly over medium heat, stirring frequently. When heated, stir in beans. Cover and cook for 2–3 minutes. Arrange on a platter and serve as directed in step 4.

CHEESY EGGPLANT AND SAUSAGE CASSEROLE

Serves 4

Approximately 9.4 g fat, 483 mg sodium per serving

Low-calorie cooking spray
2½ cups (about 10 ounces) ¼-inch slices eggplant, peeled
½ pound hot or sweet Italian turkey sausage
½ cup chopped yellow onion
1 garlic clove, minced
¼ cup no-salt tomato paste
½ cup water
3 tablespoons dry red wine
2 teaspoons sugar
½ teaspoon cinnamon
½ teaspoon dried oregano leaves
¼ teaspoon allspice
1½ cups hot cooked rice (no margarine or salt added during cooking)
2 tablespoons chopped fresh parsley
½ cup (2 ounces) shredded mozzarella cheese
⅓ cup (1½ ounces) grated provolone cheese
Paprika

1. Preheat oven to 350° F.

2. Coat a 10-inch ovenproof nonstick skillet with a low-calorie cooking spray. Over medium-high heat, brown eggplant slices on one side for 3 minutes. Turn and brown other side for 3–4 minutes. Remove from skillet and set aside.

3. In the same skillet, brown sausage, stirring frequently, about 5 minutes. Drain and discard excess grease. Place sausage on paper towels to remove additional grease. Wipe skillet dry with a paper towel.

4. In the same skillet, sauté onion and garlic over medium heat for 3 minutes. Remove from heat. Add tomato paste, water, wine, sugar, cinnamon, oregano, and allspice. Mix well. Add rice, sausage, and parsley and mix well.

5. Arrange eggplant slices on top of meat mixture. Sprinkle with mozzarella and provolone cheeses and paprika. Bake for 20–25 minutes. Let stand 10 minutes before serving.

MAKE-AHEAD MEAL DIRECTIONS

To Freeze: Complete steps 1–4 of the recipe. (Note: Do not continue to step 5.) Spread meat mixture in bottom of an 8-inch square foil pan. Arrange eggplant slices on top of meat. Sprinkle with mozzarella and provolone cheeses and paprika.

Let casserole cool completely. Wrap tightly with freezer foil and freeze. This can be kept frozen for up to 1 month.

To Prepare for Serving: Let casserole thaw completely. Preheat oven to 350° F. Unwrap casserole and bake for 30–35 minutes, or until heated thoroughly. Let stand 10 minutes before serving.

MEXICAN STUFFED PEPPERS

Serves 4

Approximately 9.4 g fat, 483 mg sodium

Low-calorie cooking spray
½ pound sweet or hot Italian turkey sausage
½ cup drained canned kidney beans, rinsed
½ cup frozen corn kernels
½ cup finely chopped yellow onion
¼ cup chopped fresh mild green chili peppers
3 tablespoons chopped fresh parsley
1 cup no-salt tomato sauce
1 tablespoon chili powder
1 teaspoon dried oregano leaves
1 teaspoon ground cumin
⅛ teaspoon hot sauce
⅓ cup cornmeal
4 green bell peppers *or* 2 red bell peppers *and* 2 yellow bell peppers with stems, seeds, and membrane removed
½ cup (2 ounces) grated reduced-fat sharp cheddar cheese

1. Preheat oven to 350° F.
2. Coat a 10-inch nonstick skillet with a low-calorie cooking spray. Over medium-high heat, brown sausage, stirring frequently, about 3–4 minutes. Drain and discard excess grease. Place sausage on paper towels to remove additional grease.
3. In the skillet or in a mixing bowl, combine sausage, beans, corn, onion, green chilis, parsley, tomato sauce, chili powder, oregano, cumin, hot sauce, and cornmeal. Toss well. Fill bell peppers.
4. Wrap each pepper in aluminum foil. Fold back foil to completely uncover top of peppers.
5. Place on foil-lined oven rack and bake for 45 minutes. Top with cheese and bake 6–8 minutes longer, or until peppers are tender.

MAKE-AHEAD MEAL DIRECTIONS

To Freeze: Complete steps 2–3 of the recipe. (Note: Do not continue to step 4.) Wrap each stuffed pepper in freezer foil. Let stuffing cool completely and freeze. This can be kept frozen for up to 1 month.

To Prepare for Serving: Let stuffed peppers thaw completely. Preheat oven to 350° F. Fold back foil to completely uncover top of peppers. Bake as directed in step 5.

AUTUMN SAUSAGE AND RICE CASSEROLE

Serves 4

Approximately 8.2 g fat, 443 mg sodium per serving

½ cup water
1 teaspoon sugar
2 cups peeled and julienned carrot
Low-calorie cooking spray
10 ounces sweet Italian turkey
  sausage
½ cup chopped celery
¾ cup chopped yellow onion
1 green bell pepper, chopped
2 cups hot cooked rice (no
  margarine or salt added during
  cooking)
1 10-ounce can low-sodium
  condensed cream of mushroom
  soup, undiluted
½ cup nonfat buttermilk
2 tablespoons chopped fresh
  parsley
¼ teaspoon garlic powder
¼ teaspoon freshly ground black
  pepper

1. Preheat oven to 350° F.
2. Bring water to a boil in a 10-inch ovenproof nonstick skillet. Add sugar and carrots. Reduce heat, cover tightly, and simmer 4 minutes or until carrots are tender but still crisp. Drain well, remove from skillet, and set aside.
3. Coat skillet with a low-calorie cooking spray. Over medium-high heat, brown sausage, stirring frequently, about 4 minutes. Drain and discard excess grease. Place sausage on paper towels to remove additional grease. Wipe skillet dry with a paper towel.
4. In the same skillet, sauté celery, onion, and green pepper about 5 minutes over medium-high heat, stirring occasionally, until vegetables are tender but still crisp. Add sausage, rice, soup, buttermilk, 1 tablespoon parsley, garlic powder, and black pepper. Blend well.
5. Arrange carrots around sausage mixture and top with remaining 1 tablespoon parsley. Bake uncovered for 20 minutes.

MAKE-AHEAD MEAL DIRECTIONS

To Freeze: Complete steps 2–4 of the recipe. (Note: Do not continue to step 5.) Place sausage mixture in an 8-inch square foil pan. Arrange carrots around sausage mixture and top with remaining 1 tablespoon parsley.

Let cool completely, wrap tightly with freezer foil, and freeze. This can be kept frozen for up to 1 month.

To Prepare for Serving: Let mixture thaw completely. Preheat oven to 350° F. Place wrapped container in oven and bake for 50–55 minutes, or until heated thoroughly.

SAUSAGE AND CHEDDAR CRUSTLESS TART

Serves 4

Approximately 9.9 g fat, 407 mg sodium per serving

7 ounces ground turkey sausage
1 large egg
3 large egg whites
⅓ cup evaporated skim milk
¼ teaspoon paprika
⅛ teaspoon black pepper
½ cup plus 2 tablespoons (2½ ounces) grated reduced-fat, low-sodium sharp cheddar cheese

1. Preheat oven to 350° F.
2. In a 10-inch ovenproof nonstick skillet, brown sausage over medium-high heat for about 3–4 minutes. Drain and discard excess grease. Place sausage on paper towels to remove additional grease. Wipe skillet dry with a paper towel.
3. In the same skillet, combine egg, egg whites, milk, paprika, and pepper. Beat well. Stir in sausage and top with cheese.
4. Bake for 25 minutes. Let stand 5 minutes before serving.

MAKE-AHEAD MEAL DIRECTIONS

To Freeze: Complete steps 1–3 of the recipe. (Note: Do not continue to step 4.) Bake for 25 minutes. Let cool completely, wrap tightly with freezer foil, and freeze. This can be kept frozen for up to 2 weeks.

To Prepare for Serving: Let tart thaw completely. Preheat oven to 350° F. Place wrapped skillet in oven and bake for 18–20 minutes, or until heated thoroughly. Let stand 5 minutes before serving.

5
✤ BEEF ✤

Sirloin in Rich Brandy Sauce with Angel Hair Pasta
Savory Braised Sirloin
Slow-Cooked Norwegian Sirloin
Marinated Sirloin with Peppers and Onions
Beef Teriyaki with Red Bell Pepper
Old-Fashioned Smothered Steak and Potatoes
Burgundy Beef Potatoes
Spicy Szechwan Beef Salad
Country-Style Vegetable Beef Soup
Stir-Fried Beef with Snow Peas
Beef Genoa
Savory Roast Beef
Po' Boys of Chartres Street
Lemon-Peppered Roast Beef
Hearty Beef Pot Pie
Roast Beef and Mixed Lettuce Salad
Mile-High Sandwiches
Hong Kong Meatballs

Spiced Meatballs with Fresh Green Beans
Beef and Potato Casserole with Three Cheeses
Barbecued Meatloaf with Fresh Corn
Meatballs in Rich Red Wine Gravy
Barcelona Beef and Rice
Lebanese Beef with Eggplant
Blue Cheese Beef and Noodle Casserole
Quick Vegetable Parmesan Soup
Tortilla Bake
Super Sloppy Joes
Baked Skillet Pizza
The Quarter-Pound Burger
Roquefort-Cheddar Beef
Beef and Corn Méxicano
Mexican Beef and Rice with Sour Cream

SIRLOIN IN RICH BRANDY SAUCE WITH ANGEL HAIR PASTA

Serves 4   **Approximately 5.0 g fat, 342 mg sodium per serving**

Juicy strips of sirloin in a hearty sauce, tossed with sautéed zucchini and mushrooms and served with pasta.

Low-calorie cooking spray
1½ cups julienned zucchini
1½ cups sliced fresh mushrooms
2 garlic cloves, minced
3 cups hot al dente–cooked angel
  hair pasta (about 6 ounces dry)
  (no salt added during cooking)
2 tablespoons chopped fresh
  parsley
¾ pound boneless sirloin, sliced
  thin and cut into 2-inch strips
½ cup beef broth (canned,
  undiluted)
¼ cup water
1 tablespoon Dijon mustard
2 tablespoons brandy
3 tablespoons evaporated skim
  milk
Dash freshly ground black pepper

1. Coat a 12-inch nonstick skillet with a low-calorie cooking spray. Sauté zucchini, mushrooms, and garlic over medium-high heat until zucchini is tender, about 5–6 minutes. Place cooked pasta on a serving platter and toss with cooked vegetables and parsley. Cover and keep warm.

2. Recoat skillet with low-calorie cooking spray. Place beef in the skillet and brown over high heat 4–5 minutes, or until liquid evaporates. Using a slotted spoon, remove beef from skillet and set aside. Reduce heat to medium-high. Add beef broth, water, and mustard to the pan drippings. Heat through, scraping the bottom and sides of the skillet. Remove from heat, add brandy, and stir well. Return skillet to medium-high, bring mixture to a boil, and cook for 1 minute.

3. Add milk and pepper to skillet. Heat thoroughly, stirring constantly, for 1–2 minutes, or until sauce is slightly thickened. (If sauce is too thick, add 1–2 tablespoons water.) Add cooked beef and any accumulated juices and stir well. Spoon beef and sauce around pasta and vegetables and serve.

MAKE-AHEAD MEAL DIRECTIONS

To Freeze: Complete step 2 of the recipe. (Note: Do not continue to step 3.) Let beef and sauce cool completely. Place mixture in a 1-quart freezer bag. Seal bag tightly, allowing no excess air to remain, and freeze. This can be kept frozen for up to 1 month.

To Prepare for Serving: Let beef mixture thaw completely. Prepare pasta and vegetables as directed in step 1 of the recipe. Place thawed beef mixture in a skillet over medium heat.

In a small glass, combine 2 teaspoons cornstarch and 2 tablespoons cold water. Stir into beef mixture and heat thoroughly, stirring occasionally. Spoon beef and sauce around pasta and vegetables, and serve.

SAVORY BRAISED SIRLOIN

Serves 4

Approximately 8.7 g fat, 485 mg sodium per serving

Low-calorie cooking spray
1 tablespoon extra-virgin olive oil
¾ pound sirloin tip, cut into 1-
  inch cubes
1 tablespoon low-sodium soy sauce
2 cups water
1 teaspoon beef bouillon granules
¼ cup dry red wine
2 garlic cloves, minced
¼ teaspoon freshly ground black
  pepper
2 cups diagonally sliced carrot
¼ teaspoon sugar
1 teaspoon cornstarch
2 cups hot cooked egg noodles
  (about 4 ounces dry) (no
  margarine or salt added during
  cooking)
3 tablespoons finely chopped
  green onion

1. Coat a dutch oven with a low-calorie cooking spray. Add olive oil and heat over high heat. Add beef and brown, stirring constantly, being careful not to scorch, about 3–4 minutes. Add soy sauce, 1 cup water, bouillon granules, wine, garlic, and black pepper. Bring to a boil, cover tightly, reduce heat, and simmer 70 minutes, or until meat is tender. Add carrots, cover tightly, and simmer 12–15 minutes longer.

2. In a small mixing bowl, combine remaining 1 cup water, sugar, and cornstarch. Mix well, add to beef mixture, and stir. Bring to a boil and stir 1 minute.

3. Place noodles on one side of a serving platter and sprinkle with green onion. Spoon beef mixture beside noodles and serve.

MAKE-AHEAD MEAL DIRECTIONS

To Freeze: Complete steps 1–2 of the recipe, omitting cornstarch. (Note: Do not continue to step 3.) Pour beef mixture into an 8-inch square foil pan. Let cool completely, wrap tightly with freezer foil, and freeze. This can be kept frozen for up to 1 month.

To Prepare for Serving: Unwrap container and let mixture thaw completely. Preheat oven to 350° F. Blend cornstarch into 2 tablespoons water and stir into mixture. Rewrap container and bake for 30 minutes, or until heated thoroughly. Serve with noodles and green onion as directed in step 3.

SLOW-COOKED NORWEGIAN SIRLOIN

Serves 4   **Approximately 6.9 g fat, 438 mg sodium per serving**

Sirloin tip, browned and slow-cooked in its juices with sweet carrots and onions, and seasoned with brandy and spices.

Low-calorie cooking spray
¾ pound boneless sirloin tip
1 teaspoon vegetable oil
3 medium carrots, cut into 2-inch
    pieces
1½ medium yellow onions, cut into
    wedges
2 teaspoons freshly grated ginger
    root
1 garlic clove, minced
1 tablespoon flour
¾ cup dry white wine
¾ cup beef broth (canned or
    homemade)
2 tablespoons brandy
1 tablespoon unsulfured molasses
1 small bay leaf
1 teaspoon ground coriander
⅛ teaspoon ground red pepper
2 cups hot cooked egg noodles
    (about 4 ounces dry) (no
    margarine or salt added during
    cooking)
½ teaspoon poppy seeds
2 tablespoons chopped fresh
    parsley

1. Preheat oven to 325° F.
2. Coat an ovenproof dutch oven, preferably cast-iron, with a low-calorie cooking spray. Over medium heat, brown meat on all sides, about 5 minutes. Remove meat and set aside. Add oil and increase heat to medium-high. When oil is heated, add carrots and onions to pot. Cook, stirring frequently, until lightly browned, about 5–8 minutes. Add ginger and garlic and cook 30 seconds longer.
3. In a mixing bowl, whisk together flour, wine, beef broth, brandy, molasses, bay leaf, coriander, and red pepper. Add to the vegetables in the dutch oven and bring to a boil. Add beef, cover tightly, and bake for 2 hours, or until beef is tender. Remove and discard bay leaf.
4. Place beef mixture in the center of a serving platter. Toss noodles with poppy seeds and arrange around beef mixture. Sprinkle fresh parsley over all.

MAKE-AHEAD MEAL DIRECTIONS

To Freeze: Complete steps 1–3 of the recipe. (Note: Do not continue to step 4.) Pour beef mixture into an 8-inch square foil pan. Let cool completely, wrap tightly with freezer foil, and freeze. This can be kept frozen for up to 1 month.

To Prepare for Serving: Let mixture thaw completely. Preheat oven to 350° F. Place wrapped container in oven and bake for 40–45 minutes, or until heated thoroughly. Serve with noodles as directed in step 4.

MARINATED SIRLOIN WITH PEPPERS AND ONIONS

Serves 4

Approximately 9.1 g fat, 487 mg sodium per serving

2 tablespoons minced yellow onion
¼ cup water
¼ cup dry red wine
3 tablespoons low-sodium soy sauce
2 tablespoons fresh lime juice
1 teaspoon Dijon mustard
1½ tablespoons extra-virgin olive oil
2 tablespoons chopped fresh parsley
1 tablespoon low-sodium Worcestershire sauce
2 garlic cloves, minced
½ teaspoon freshly ground black pepper
¾ pound boneless top round, cut into bite-sized pieces
Low-calorie cooking spray
2 cups cooked rice (no margarine or salt added during cooking)
1 large green bell pepper, cut into 1-inch pieces
1 medium yellow onion, cut into eighths and layers separated
Paprika

1. In a mixing bowl, combine minced onion, water, wine, soy sauce, lime juice, mustard, olive oil, parsley, Worcestershire sauce, garlic, and black pepper. Mix well and add beef. Cover and marinate in the refrigerator overnight, or at least 2 hours, stirring occasionally.

2. Preheat oven to 350° F.

3. Coat the bottom of 2-quart casserole dish with a low-calorie cooking spray. Spread rice on bottom of casserole. Top with meat and marinade, green pepper, and onion pieces. Sprinkle with paprika, cover tightly, and bake for 40 minutes.

MAKE-AHEAD MEAL DIRECTIONS

To Freeze: Prepare marinade and add beef as directed in step 1 of the recipe. (Note: Do not marinate in refrigerator or continue to step 2.) Place beef and marinade in a 1-quart freezer bag. Seal bag tightly, allowing no excess air to remain, and freeze. This can be kept frozen for up to 2 weeks.

To Prepare for Serving: Let beef mixture thaw completely. Prepare casserole as directed in steps 2–3 of the recipe.

BEEF TERIYAKI WITH RED BELL PEPPER

Serves 4   **Approximately 6.2 g fat, 485 mg sodium per serving**

Sirloin marinated and then braised in a bold bourbon-teriyaki sauce, served on a bed of rice with red bell peppers and onions.

2½ tablespoons low-sodium soy
   sauce
¼ cup bourbon
3 tablespoons dark brown sugar,
   packed
1 tablespoon Dijon mustard
2 garlic cloves
½ teaspoon black pepper
1 pound boneless sirloin, all fat
   removed, cut into 1-inch pieces
Low-calorie cooking spray
1 red bell pepper, cut into 1-inch
   pieces
1 yellow onion, cut into eighths,
   layers separated
2 cups hot cooked rice (no
   margarine or salt added during
   cooking)
¼ cup water

1. In a 1-gallon freezer bag, combine soy sauce, bourbon, brown sugar, mustard, garlic, and black pepper. Mix thoroughly and add beef. Seal bag, releasing any excess air. Shake to coat beef thoroughly. Marinate in refrigerator overnight.

2. Coat a 12-inch nonstick skillet with a low-calorie cooking spray. Heat 1 minute over medium-high heat, add red pepper and onion, and sauté 5–6 minutes, or until edges begin to brown. Cover and cook 5–6 minutes longer until tender-crisp. Mound hot cooked rice on a serving platter and spoon vegetables around rice. Cover and keep warm.

3. Recoat skillet with low-calorie cooking spray. Heat 1 minute over high heat. Remove beef from marinade, reserving marinade, and place in hot skillet. Cook 5–6 minutes, stirring constantly, until liquid has evaporated and a glaze develops. Remove beef from skillet and set aside. Add water to skillet and scrape down sides and bottom of skillet. Boil 1 minute. Add marinade and beef, and cook over high heat 3–4 minutes longer or until marinade reaches consistency of a rich glaze. Spoon glazed meat over rice.

MAKE-AHEAD MEAL DIRECTIONS

To Freeze: Prepare marinade and coat beef as directed in step 1 of the recipe. Freeze instead of marinating. (Note: Do not continue to step 2.) This can be kept frozen for up to 1 month.

To Prepare for Serving: Let beef mixture thaw completely. Shake to blend seasonings. Complete steps 2–3 of the recipe.

OLD-FASHIONED SMOTHERED STEAK AND POTATOES

Serves 4

Approximately 9.7 g fat, 470 mg sodium per serving

2 8-ounce baking potatoes
Low-calorie cooking spray
1 pound sirloin steak, cut into
    fourths
¼ teaspoon garlic powder
½ teaspoon salt (if desired)
1 tablespoon butter
1 medium yellow onion, sliced
1 cup sliced fresh mushrooms
1 medium green bell pepper,
    sliced
¼ teaspoon black pepper
2 teaspoons butter substitute (I use
    Molly McButter)
Freshly ground black pepper

1. Preheat oven to 350° F.

2. Wrap potatoes individually in aluminum foil. Bake for 1 hour.

3. While potatoes are baking, coat a 12-inch nonstick skillet (preferably cast-iron) with a low-calorie cooking spray. Over high heat, add meat and garlic powder, and cook 2½ minutes. Turn meat, sprinkle with ¼ teaspoon salt, and cook 2½–3 minutes longer. Place meat on a serving platter and keep warm.

4. Dry skillet with paper towels. Reduce heat to medium-high, add butter, and heat until bubbly. Add onion, mushrooms, and green pepper, and cook about 6–8 minutes, stirring frequently, until edges brown. Stir in remaining ¼ teaspoon salt and black pepper. Spoon vegetable mixture over meat.

5. Split potatoes in half and fluff with a fork. Sprinkle each with ½ teaspoon butter substitute and black pepper. Arrange around meat on serving platter.

Do Not Freeze

BURGUNDY BEEF POTATOES

Serves 4   Approximately 5.1 g fat, 438 mg sodium

Potatoes stuffed with beef in a hearty burgundy-mushroom sauce.

4 8-ounce baking potatoes
Low-calorie cooking spray
½ pound top round steak, cut into
   thin strips
1 teaspoon butter
4 cups sliced fresh mushrooms
½ cup thinly sliced yellow onion
1 cup beef broth (canned,
   undiluted)
2 tablespoons chopped green
   onion
2 tablespoons chopped fresh
   parsley
1 small bay leaf
½ teaspoon sugar
¼ teaspoon low-sodium
   Worcestershire sauce
2 tablespoons dry red wine
1 tablespoon cornstarch
Freshly ground black pepper

1. Preheat oven to 350° F.
2. Wrap potatoes individually in aluminum foil. Bake for 1 hour.
3. While potatoes are baking, coat a 10-inch nonstick skillet with a low-calorie cooking spray. Over medium-high heat, brown beef about 3–4 minutes, or until slightly pink inside. Drain and discard excess grease. Place beef on paper towels to remove additional grease. Wipe skillet dry with a paper towel.
4. Melt butter in skillet. Add mushrooms and onion, and sauté until liquid is absorbed, about 5–6 minutes. Add beef, beef broth, green onion, parsley, bay leaf, sugar, and Worcestershire sauce. In a small glass, combine wine with cornstarch. Mix well, and add to skillet. Bring to boil and cook 1–2 minutes until sauce is slightly thickened. Remove from heat. Remove and discard bay leaf.
5. Split potatoes in half. Gently fluff potatoes with a fork, being careful not to tear the outer skin. Spoon equal portions of beef and mushroom sauce over each potato. Top with freshly ground black pepper.

Variation: For a meatless entree, omit beef and otherwise make as directed. This variation provides only 1.8 grams of fat and 414 milligrams sodium.

MAKE-AHEAD MEAL DIRECTIONS

To Freeze: Prepare beef and sauce as directed in steps 3–4 of the recipe, omitting cornstarch. Sauce will not be thickened. (Note: Do not continue to step 5.)
   Let beef mixture cool completely. Place in a 1-quart freezer bag. Seal bag tightly, allowing no excess air to remain, and freeze. This can be kept frozen for up to 1 month.
   To Prepare for Serving: Let beef mixture thaw completely. Bake potatoes as directed in steps 1–2 of the recipe. While potatoes are baking, pour beef mixture into a medium saucepan. Blend cornstarch with ¼ cup water and add to beef mixture, stirring well. Heat thoroughly over medium heat. Cook until sauce is slightly thickened but no longer than 10 minutes. Serve with potatoes as directed in step 5.

SPICY SZECHWAN BEEF SALAD

Serves 4   Approximately 9.6 g fat, 255 mg sodium per serving

Beef marinated in brown sugar, soy sauce, orange juice, and spices, then stir-fried with shredded romaine.

3 tablespoons dark brown sugar, packed
2 tablespoons low-sodium soy sauce
2 tablespoons orange juice
2 teaspoons orange zest
1/4 teaspoon ginger root
1/2 red pepper flakes
1/2 teaspoon dry mustard
1/2 teaspoon chili powder
1 pound top round, thinly sliced diagonally
Low-calorie cooking spray
2 teaspoons sesame or peanut oil
1 green bell pepper, thinly sliced
2 ounces snow peas
1 green onion, chopped
8 cups shredded romaine lettuce
1 tablespoon unsalted peanuts

1. In a 1-gallon freezer bag, combine sugar, soy sauce, orange juice, orange zest, ginger root, red pepper flakes, dry mustard, and chili powder. Mix thoroughly and add beef. Seal bag, releasing any excess air. Shake to coat beef thoroughly. Marinate in refrigerator at least 2 hours.

2. Shake beef mixture well.

3. Heat a wok or 12-inch nonstick skillet coated with a low-calorie cooking spray 1 minute over high heat. Add beef and stir-fry 3 minutes, or until no longer pink. Remove beef and set aside. Add oil to wok or skillet. Add green pepper, snow peas, and green onion. Stir-fry 2 minutes. Return beef to wok or skillet, add lettuce and peanuts, and toss until thoroughly heated. Serve immediately.

MAKE-AHEAD MEAL DIRECTIONS

To Freeze: Prepare marinade and coat beef as directed in step 1 of the recipe. Freeze instead of marinating. (Note: Do not continue to step 2.) This can be kept frozen for up to 1 month.

To Prepare for Serving: Let beef mixture thaw completely. Complete steps 2–3 of the recipe.

COUNTRY-STYLE VEGETABLE BEEF SOUP

Serves 4

Approximately 8.8 g fat, 496 mg sodium per serving

Low-calorie cooking spray
1 pound bottom round steak,
   trimmed of all fat and cut into
   bite-sized pieces
1 medium yellow onion, chopped
2 garlic cloves, minced
1 teaspoon low-sodium beef
   bouillon granules
1 16-ounce can chopped tomatoes,
   undrained
½ cup unsalted tomato sauce
4 cups water
1 small bay leaf
1 teaspoon sugar
¼ teaspoon freshly ground black
   pepper
⅛ teaspoon prepared hot pepper
   sauce
2 cups chopped cabbage
1 cup 2-inch-long pieces fresh
   green beans
½ cup sliced carrots
¾ cup chopped celery
½ cup frozen corn kernels
¼ cup chopped green bell pepper
2 tablespoons chopped fresh
   parsley
1 teaspoon salt (if desired)

1. Coat the bottom and sides of a dutch oven, preferably cast-iron, with a low-calorie cooking spray. Add beef, onion, and garlic and brown over medium-high heat for about 3–4 minutes.

2. Add beef bouillon granules, tomatoes, tomato sauce, water, bay leaf, sugar, black pepper, and hot pepper sauce. Bring to a boil, cover, reduce heat, and simmer 1 hour. Add cabbage, green beans, carrots, celery, corn, green pepper, and parsley. Bring to a boil, reduce heat, cover tightly, and simmer 30 minutes longer. Add salt and remove bay leaf before serving. To enhance flavor, refrigerate soup overnight.

MAKE-AHEAD MEAL DIRECTIONS

To Freeze: Complete steps 1–2 of the recipe. Let soup cool completely. Place in two 1-gallon freezer bags. Seal bags tightly, allowing no excess air to remain, and freeze. This can be kept frozen for up to 1 month.

To Prepare for Serving: Let soup thaw completely. Pour into a dutch oven. Cover and heat thoroughly over medium heat, stirring occasionally.

STIR-FRIED BEEF WITH SNOW PEAS

Serves 4

Approximately 8.8 g fat, 229 mg sodium per serving

¼ cup fresh lime juice
½ teaspoon garlic powder
2 tablespoons chopped fresh
   parsley
½ teaspoon red pepper flakes
⅜ teaspoon freshly ground black
   pepper
1 pound top round steak
Low-calorie cooking spray
2 teaspoons sesame oil
¾ pound fresh or frozen pea pods
1 cup thinly sliced yellow onion
⅛ teaspoon salt (if desired)
1 tablespoon sesame seeds, toasted
   under broiler
1 tablespoon cornstarch
½ cup water
1 tablespoon low-sodium soy sauce
Cracked pepper

1. In a 1-gallon freezer bag, combine lime juice, ¼ teaspoon garlic powder, parsley, red pepper flakes, and ¼ teaspoon black pepper. Mix thoroughly and add beef. Seal bag, releasing any excess air. Turn over several times to coat beef thoroughly. Marinate in refrigerator overnight.

2. In a nonaluminum skillet, heat 2 teaspoons oil and ¼ teaspoon garlic powder 1 minute over medium-high heat. Add pea pods, onion, and salt, and stir-fry 5 minutes. Add sesame seeds. Toss well and cook 1–2 minutes longer, or until pea pods are tender but still crisp. Spoon vegetables into center of a serving platter and place in a warm oven uncovered.

3. Slice beef into thin strips, reserving marinade. Toss meat with cornstarch. Coat skillet with low-calorie cooking spray and heat 1 minute over high heat. Add half of the beef and stir-fry 3–4 minutes. Remove meat from pan and set aside. Coat skillet again with cooking spray and repeat process with remaining meat. Return reserved meat to skillet and add water, soy sauce, and marinade. Stir and cook 2–3 minutes longer, or until sauce is thickened.

4. Spoon meat and sauce around pea pods. Top with cracked pepper and serve immediately.

MAKE-AHEAD MEAL DIRECTIONS

To Freeze: Prepare marinade and coat beef as directed in step 1 of the recipe. Freeze instead of marinating. (Note: Do not continue to step 2.) This can be kept frozen for up to 1 month.

To Prepare for Serving: Let beef mixture thaw completely. Shake to blend seasonings. Complete steps 2–4 of the recipe.

❧ ❧

BEEF GENOA

Serves 4   **Approximately 6.0 g fat, 343 mg sodium per serving**

Succulent top round simmered with Italian herbs and spices and served with spinach pasta.

1 pound boneless top round steak
2 cups sliced fresh mushrooms
⅓ cup dry red wine
⅛ teaspoon freshly ground black pepper
Low-calorie cooking spray
¼ cup tomato sauce
3 tablespoons chopped green onion
1 garlic clove, minced
¼ teaspoon sugar
1 small bay leaf
½ cup beef broth (canned, undiluted)
1½ teaspoons cornstarch
1 tablespoon chopped fresh parsley
2 cups hot cooked spinach noodles (about 4 ounces dry) (no salt added during cooking)
3 tablespoons finely chopped red onion
Freshly ground black pepper

1. In a 1-gallon freezer bag, combine mushrooms, wine, and black pepper. Mix thoroughly and add beef. Seal bag, releasing any excess air. Turn over several times to coat beef thoroughly. Marinate in refrigerator, overnight or at least 2 hours.

2. Coat a 10-inch nonstick skillet with a low-calorie cooking spray. Over medium-high heat, add beef, reserving marinade and mushrooms. Brown 4 minutes on each side. Remove skillet from heat. Remove beef from pan, slice thin, and arrange on serving platter.

3. In a mixing bowl, combine marinade, tomato sauce, green onion, garlic, sugar, bay leaf, beef broth, cornstarch, and parsley. Mix well. Add to pan drippings and bring to a boil over medium-high heat. Boil 2–3 minutes, stirring constantly, until slightly thickened. Add mushrooms to sauce and cook 3–4 minutes longer.

4. Remove bay leaf and spoon sauce over meat. Arrange hot noodles around meat and sprinkle with red onion. Top all with freshly ground black pepper.

Do Not Freeze

❧ ❧

SAVORY ROAST BEEF

Serves 4

Approximately 5.7 g fat, 438 mg sodium per serving

1 tablespoon flour
1 medium browning bag
1¼ pounds eye of round roast
8 small new potatoes (about 1 ounce each)
2 medium yellow onions, quartered
2 medium carrots, peeled and cut into 1-inch pieces
1 cup 2-inch-long pieces fresh green beans
1 celery stalk, cut into 3-inch pieces
¼ teaspoon beef bouillon granules
¼ teaspoon black pepper
¼ teaspoon garlic powder
½ teaspoon paprika

1. Preheat oven to 350° F.
2. Place flour in a browning bag and shake well. Add beef to bag, along with potatoes, onions, carrots, green beans, and celery. Sprinkle beef bouillon granules, black pepper, garlic powder, and paprika over all. Seal bag with a tie and place in an 8″ × 12″ baking pan.
3. Make 6 ½-inch slits in the top of the bag and bake for 1 hour and 15 minutes. Carefully remove wrapping and let beef stand for 7–8 minutes. Thinly slice beef and arrange on a serving platter with vegetables.

MAKE-AHEAD MEAL DIRECTIONS

To Freeze: Complete step 2 of the recipe, except do not place bag in baking pan. Wrap bagged beef and vegetables in freezer foil for extra protection. This can be kept frozen for up to 1 month.

To Prepare for Serving: Let meat and vegetables thaw completely. Preheat oven to 350° F. Remove foil from browning bag and place bag in an 8″ × 12″ baking pan. Bake and serve as directed in step 3 of the recipe.

PO' BOYS OF CHARTRES STREET

Serves 4   **Approximately 7.7 g fat, 451 mg sodium per serving**

Crusty French rolls filled with slices of beef in a rich brown gravy.

1¼ pounds eye of round roast
1 cup plus 2 tablespoons water
½ teaspoon beef bouillon granules
1 teaspoon low-sodium
    Worcestershire sauce
⅛ teaspoon black pepper
¼ teaspoon garlic powder
1 tablespoon cornstarch
4 1½-ounce French bread rolls
2 teaspoons Dijon mustard
¼ small red onion, thinly sliced
    and separated into rings
1 green bell pepper, cut into thin
    strips
1 medium tomato, thinly sliced
1 cup shredded green or red
    cabbage

1. Preheat oven to 325° F.

2. Place meat on a baking rack and bake 1 hour and 15 minutes. Remove from oven and let stand 15 minutes.

3. Slice beef thin and place in a medium saucepan. Add 1 cup water, beef bouillon granules, Worcestershire sauce, black pepper, and garlic powder. Bring to a boil, reduce heat, cover tightly, and simmer 10 minutes.

4. In a small glass, combine cornstarch and 2 tablespoons water. Mix well and stir into pan. Increase heat to high and boil 1 minute uncovered, or until sauce is thickened.

5. Split each roll in half and hollow out, leaving only the outer shell. Place in 350° F oven for 2 minutes to warm, if desired. Spoon ½ teaspoon mustard on bottom half of each roll. Spoon equal amounts of beef into rolls. Top each with onion, green pepper, tomato, and cabbage. Cover with the top half. Arrange sandwiches on serving platter and serve immediately.

MAKE-AHEAD MEAL DIRECTIONS

To Freeze: Prepare beef as directed in steps 1–3 of the recipe. Let beef mixture cool completely. Place in a 1-quart freezer bag. Seal bag tightly, allowing no excess air to remain, and freeze. This can be kept frozen for up to 1 month.

To Prepare for Serving: Let beef mixture thaw completely. Preheat oven to 350° F. Place beef mixture in a medium saucepan and heat thoroughly over medium heat. Complete steps 4–5 of the recipe.

LEMON-PEPPERED ROAST BEEF

Serves 4

Approximately 6.3 g fat, 475 mg sodium per serving

1 pound eye of round, all fat
  removed
Low-calorie cooking spray
5 garlic cloves, peeled and left
  whole
½ teaspoon lemon pepper
4 6-ounce baking potatoes
½ cup light sour cream
¼ cup chopped green onion tops
⅛ teaspoon salt (if desired)
⅛ teaspoon black pepper

1. Preheat oven to 325° F.
2. Place beef on a broiler rack coated with a low-calorie cooking spray. Make five 1-inch slits around beef and stuff each with a garlic clove. Sprinkle roast with lemon pepper.
3. Place potatoes in oven with meat and bake 1 hour.
4. Remove meat and potatoes. Let beef stand 6–8 minutes, then slice thin.
5. Split potatoes in half and top each half with equal amounts of sour cream, green onion, salt, and pepper.

MAKE-AHEAD MEAL DIRECTIONS

To Freeze: Make five 1-inch slits around beef and stuff each with a garlic clove. Sprinkle roast with lemon pepper. Place in a 1-gallon freezer bag. Seal bag tightly, allowing no excess air to remain, and freeze. This can be kept frozen for up to 1 month.

To Prepare for Serving: Let beef thaw completely. Preheat oven to 325° F. Place beef on a broiler rack coated with a low-calorie cooking spray. Roast beef and bake potatoes as directed in steps 3–4 of the recipe. Complete step 5.

HEARTY BEEF POT PIE

Serves 4

Approximately 6.8 g fat, 497 mg sodium per serving

4 teaspoons unsalted butter
1 cup canned beef broth
1 cup water
⅔ cup flour
8 ounces eye of round, all fat removed, cut into ½-inch cubes
1 6-ounce potato, peeled and diced into ¼-inch cubes
1 cup matchstick-sized pieces carrot
⅓ cup finely chopped yellow onion
¼ teaspoon black pepper
⅛ teaspoon garlic powder
1 teaspoon low-sodium Worcestershire sauce
1 tablespoon plus 1 teaspoon vegetable oil
1 tablespoon plus 1 teaspoon nonfat buttermilk
½ teaspoon poppy seeds (if desired)

1. Preheat oven to 425° F.
2. In a 10-inch nonstick skillet, melt butter over medium-high heat. Add beef broth and water. Whisk in 2 tablespoons flour, bring to a boil, and cook, stirring with a flat spatula, about 4–5 minutes or until thickened. Remove from heat. Stir in beef, potatoes, carrot, onion, black pepper, garlic powder, and Worcestershire sauce. Spoon mixture into an 8-inch square pan.
3. Combine ½ cup flour, oil, and buttermilk. Blend well. Place on a fairly large sheet of plastic wrap, about 16 inches long. Top dough with another sheet of plastic wrap. Press down with rolling pin and roll out dough to make a thin pie crust.
4. Place pie crust on top of pot pie and sprinkle evenly with poppy seeds, if desired. Bake for 45–50 minutes, until crust is golden. Let stand 10 minutes before serving.

MAKE-AHEAD MEAL DIRECTIONS

To Freeze: Complete steps 2–3 of the recipe, omitting potatoes. (Note: Do not continue to step 4.) Let meat mixture cool completely and stir in potatoes. Place crust on top of pie and sprinkle with poppy seeds, if desired.

Wrap tightly with freezer foil and freeze. This can be kept frozen for up to 1 month.

To Prepare for Serving: Do not thaw. Preheat oven to 425° F. Unwrap frozen pie and bake 55–60 minutes, or until crust is golden. Let stand 10 minutes before serving.

ROAST BEEF AND MIXED LETTUCE SALAD

Serves 4

Approximately 9.9 g fat, 422 mg sodium per serving

12 ounces boneless top sirloin, all fat removed
Low-calorie cooking spray
2 tablespoons dry red wine
2 tablespoons low-sodium soy sauce
2 tablespoons water
2 tablespoons fresh lime juice
1 tablespoon extra-virgin olive oil
2 tablespoons chopped fresh parsley
1½ teaspoons low-sodium Worcestershire sauce
½ teaspoon dried oregano leaves
¼ teaspoon dried basil leaves
¼ teaspoon black pepper
⅛ teaspoon garlic powder
4 cups torn red-leaf lettuce
4 cups torn romaine lettuce
1 cup sliced fresh mushrooms
½ cup slivered red or green bell pepper
½ small red onion, thinly sliced and separated into rings
1 medium tomato, cut into wedges
½ cucumber, peeled and thinly sliced
¼ cup (1 ounce) grated provolone cheese

1. Preheat broiler.
2. Place beef on a broiler rack coated with a low-calorie cooking spray. Broil for 3 minutes on each side 2–3 inches away from heat source. Let cool, then cut into strips.
3. In a 1-quart freezer bag, combine wine, soy sauce, water, lime juice, olive oil, parsley, Worcestershire sauce, oregano, basil, black pepper, and garlic powder. Mix thoroughly and add beef. Seal bag, releasing any excess air. Shake to coat beef thoroughly. Marinate in refrigerator 2 hours or at least 30 minutes.
4. Place red-leaf and romaine lettuce in a salad bowl. Arrange mushrooms, red or green pepper, onion, tomato, and cucumber on top of lettuce. Place beef and marinade in center of salad. Top with provolone cheese. Toss well and serve immediately.

MAKE-AHEAD MEAL DIRECTIONS

To Freeze: Cook beef as directed in steps 1–2 of the recipe. Prepare marinade and coat beef as directed in step 3. Freeze instead of marinating. (Note: Do not continue to step 4.) This can be kept frozen for up to 2 weeks.

To Prepare for Serving: Let beef and marinade thaw completely. Shake to blend seasonings. Assemble salad as directed in step 4 of the recipe.

MILE-HIGH SANDWICHES

Serves 4

Approximately 7.9 g fat, 455 mg sodium per serving

1 pound eye of round, all fat removed
¼ teaspoon salt (if desired)
⅛ teaspoon pepper
⅛ teaspoon garlic powder
Low-calorie cooking spray
2 tablespoons country-style Dijon mustard
1 tablespoon nonfat plain yogurt
1 tablespoon reduced-calorie mayonnaise
½ teaspoon dried dill weed (if desired)
8 pieces reduced-calorie Italian bread
4 lettuce leaves
2 medium tomatoes, cut into 8 slices
8 thinly sliced red onion rings
8 thinly sliced red or green bell pepper rings
½ cup alfalfa sprouts
Freshly ground black pepper, to taste

1. Preheat oven to 325° F.
2. Sprinkle beef with salt, pepper, and garlic powder. Place on a broiler rack coated with a low-calorie cooking spray. Bake for 55 minutes. Let beef stand for 15 minutes, then slice thin.
3. In a small mixing bowl, combine mustard, yogurt, mayonnaise, and dill. Blend well. Spread 1½ teaspoons on each slice of bread.
4. On each of four slices, place 3 ounces beef, 1 lettuce leaf, 2 tomato slices, 2 onion rings, 2 bell pepper rings, and 2 tablespoons alfalfa sprouts. Grind pepper over sprouts, then top with remaining four slices of bread. Cut sandwiches in half and serve immediately.

Do Not Freeze

HONG KONG MEATBALLS

Serves 4

Approximately 6.3 g fat, 335 mg sodium

1 pound lean ground round
2 slices reduced-calorie bread, toasted and grated
½ cup finely chopped yellow onion
1 teaspoon cornstarch
2 egg whites
¼ teaspoon freshly ground black pepper
3 tablespoons skim milk
1 teaspoon anise seed (if desired)
Low-calorie cooking spray
¼ cup water
Juice from 1 large orange
½ teaspoon orange zest
2 tablespoons low-sodium soy sauce
¼ cup prepared chili sauce
¼ cup low-sugar grape jelly
2 cups hot cooked rice (no margarine or salt added during cooking)

1. Combine ground beef, bread crumbs, onion, cornstarch, egg whites, black pepper, milk, and anise in a large mixing bowl. Mix well and form into 40 1-inch balls. Chill 30 minutes.

2. Coat a 12-inch nonstick skillet with a low-calorie cooking spray. Over high heat, brown meatballs on all sides, 5–6 minutes. Drain and discard excess grease. Place meatballs on paper towels to remove additional grease.

3. Heat water in skillet and boil 1 minute, scraping bottom with flat spatula. Return meatballs to skillet with orange juice, orange zest, and soy sauce. Bring to a boil, cover tightly, reduce heat, and simmer 20 minutes.

4. In a small mixing bowl, combine chili sauce and grape jelly. Mix thoroughly, spoon over meatballs. Gently toss, increase heat to medium-high, and cook uncovered 7–8 minutes longer, stirring occasionally. Serve with rice.

MAKE-AHEAD MEAL DIRECTIONS

To Freeze: Complete steps 1–3 of the recipe. (Note: Do not continue to step 4.) Let meatballs cool completely. Place in a 1-gallon freezer bag. Seal bag tightly, allowing no excess air to remain, and freeze. This can be kept frozen for up to 1 month.

To Prepare for Serving: Let mixture thaw completely. Pour into dutch oven and heat thoroughly over medium heat. Complete step 4 of the recipe.

SPICED MEATBALLS WITH FRESH GREEN BEANS

Serves 4

Approximately 5.1 g fat, 470 mg sodium per serving

1 cup water
3 cups 2-inch-long pieces fresh
    green beans
¾ pound lean ground round
½ cup uncooked white rice
1 tablespoon finely chopped
    yellow onion
2 tablespoons finely chopped
    green bell pepper
1 garlic clove, minced
⅛ teaspoon ground ginger
⅛ teaspoon nutmeg
1¼ cups tomato juice
4 whole cloves
2 tablespoons cinnamon
1 tablespoon sugar
1 tablespoon low-sodium
    Worcestershire sauce
¼ teaspoon salt (if desired)

1. In a 10-inch nonstick skillet, bring water to a boil. Add green beans, reduce heat to medium-low, cover tightly, and simmer 12–15 minutes, or until beans are tender but still crisp. Drain well and set aside.

2. In a mixing bowl, mix together ground beef, rice, onion, green pepper, garlic, ginger, and nutmeg. Roll into 24 small balls and place in skillet. Spread green beans around meatballs. In a separate bowl, combine tomato juice, cloves, cinnamon, sugar, Worcestershire sauce, and salt. Pour over meatballs and beans.

3. Cover tightly and simmer for 50–60 minutes, or until meatballs are cooked. Discard cloves and serve.

MAKE-AHEAD MEAL DIRECTIONS

To Freeze: Complete steps 1–2 of the recipe. (Note: Do not continue to step 3.) Place mixture in an 8-inch square foil pan. Let cool completely, wrap tightly with freezer foil, and freeze. This can be kept frozen for up to 1 month.

To Prepare for Serving: Let mixture thaw completely. Preheat oven to 350° F. Place wrapped container in oven and bake for 70 minutes. Transfer mixture to a serving platter, discard cloves, and serve.

❧ ☙

BEEF AND POTATO CASSEROLE WITH THREE CHEESES

Serves 4

Approximately 9.9 g fat, 332 mg sodium per serving

½ pound lean ground round
½ pound fresh mushrooms,
  quartered
2 garlic cloves, minced
1 teaspoon low-sodium
  Worcestershire sauce
1 tablespoon Dijon mustard
Low-calorie cooking spray
9 small new potatoes
  (approximately 1 ounce each),
  thinly sliced
1 teaspoon extra-virgin olive oil
½ teaspoon dried dill weed
1½ ounces blue cheese, crumbled
¼ cup (1 ounce) shredded
  mozzarella cheese
¼ cup (1 ounce) grated reduced-fat
  sharp cheddar cheese
Paprika
3 tablespoons chopped fresh
  parsley

1. Preheat oven to 350° F.
2. In a 10-inch ovenproof nonstick skillet, brown ground beef over medium-high heat for about 3 minutes. Drain and discard excess grease. Place beef on paper towels to remove additional grease. Wipe skillet dry with a paper towel. Place mushrooms and garlic in the skillet and brown for about 5 minutes. Toss with Worcestershire sauce and mustard, and set aside with beef.
3. Coat the skillet with a low-calorie cooking spray. Arrange potatoes on the bottom and slightly up the sides of the skillet. Sprinkle with olive oil and dill. Bake, covered, for 30 minutes. Spread beef and mushrooms on top of potatoes. Top with cheeses and sprinkle with paprika and parsley.
4. Bake uncovered for 5–8 minutes longer, or until cheeses melt and potatoes are tender.

Variation: In place of the blue cheese, use ½ cup (2 ounces) grated Swiss cheese.

MAKE-AHEAD MEAL DIRECTIONS

To Freeze: Complete steps 2–3 of the recipe. (Note: Do not continue to step 4.) Let casserole cool completely. Wrap skillet in freezer foil and freeze. This can be kept frozen for up to 1 month.

To Prepare for Serving: Let casserole thaw completely. Preheat oven to 350° F. Place wrapped skillet in oven and bake for 25 minutes, or until thoroughly heated.

BARBECUED MEATLOAF WITH FRESH CORN

Serves 4   Approximately 7.6 g fat, 421 mg sodium per serving

1 pound lean ground round
2 tablespoons rolled oats
¼ cup finely chopped yellow onion
¼ cup chopped green bell pepper
1 egg white
½ teaspoon low-sodium
    Worcestershire sauce
¼ teaspoon garlic powder
¼ teaspoon black pepper
Low-calorie cooking spray
3 medium ears of corn, cut into
    fourths
¼ cup hickory smoked barbecue
    sauce
1 tablespoon plus 1 teaspoon low-
    calorie melted margarine
½ teaspoon lemon pepper

1. Preheat oven to 350° F.

2. In a mixing bowl, combine ground beef with oats, onion, green pepper, egg white, Worcestershire sauce, garlic powder and black pepper. Blend thoroughly. Mold meat mixture into an oval shape for meatloaf.

3. Coat a broiler rack with a low-calorie cooking spray. Place meatloaf on broiler rack.

4. Place 3 pieces of corn on a sheet of aluminum foil and wrap tightly. Repeat process to make 4 individual bundles. Bake corn and meatloaf for 35 minutes. Spoon barbecue sauce over meatloaf and continue baking with corn 10 minutes longer.

5. Roll back foil and drizzle 1 teaspoon of the melted margarine over each bundle of corn. Sprinkle lemon pepper over all and serve in foil.

MAKE-AHEAD MEAL DIRECTIONS

To Freeze: Complete step 2 of the recipe. (Note: Do not continue to step 3.) Place meatloaf in an 8-inch square foil pan and wrap tightly with freezer foil, or place in a 1-gallon freezer bag and seal tightly, squeezing out all excess air. Freeze. This can be kept frozen for up to 1 month.

To Prepare for Serving: Let meatloaf thaw completely. Preheat oven to 350° F. Complete steps 3–5 of the recipe.

MEATBALLS IN RICH RED WINE GRAVY

Serves 4

Approximately 7.0 g fat, 433 mg sodium per serving

3 tablespoons flour
1 pound lean ground round
2 slices reduced-calorie bread, toasted and grated
½ cup finely chopped yellow onion
1 teaspoon cornstarch
½ teaspoon allspice
2 egg whites
¼ teaspoon freshly ground black pepper
3 tablespoons plus ¼ cup skim milk
Low-calorie cooking spray
¾ cup condensed beef broth
1 cup water
⅛ teaspoon garlic powder
¾ teaspoon sugar
2 tablespoons dry red wine
1 cup hot cooked rice (no margarine or salt added during cooking)

1. Place flour in a 10-inch ovenproof skillet. Over medium heat, stir until flour turns from white to off-white in color, about 7–8 minutes. Remove from heat immediately and set flour aside on foil.

2. In a mixing bowl, combine beef, bread crumbs, onion, cornstarch, allspice, egg whites, black pepper, and 3 tablespoons skim milk. Chill for 30 minutes.

3. Preheat oven to 350° F.

4. Form meat mixture into 40 1-inch balls. Coat the skillet with a low-calorie cooking spray and heat 1 minute over medium-high heat. Brown meatballs 3–4 minutes, turning occasionally. Remove from pan. Add broth to pan drippings, scraping bottom and sides of pan. Whisk in flour. Add water, ¼ cup skim milk, garlic powder, sugar, and wine. Bring to a boil, cook 1 minute, then add meatballs. Remove from heat.

5. Cover skillet tightly and bake for 35 minutes. Gently stir in rice and serve.

Variation: At the end of step 4, stir in 1 cup frozen green peas and pearl onions. Omit rice in step 5. Each serving will contain approximately 7.0 grams fat and 468 milligrams sodium.

MAKE-AHEAD MEAL DIRECTIONS

To Freeze: Complete steps 1, 2, and 4 of the recipe. (Note: Do not continue to step 5.) Transfer meatballs and gravy to an 8-inch square foil pan. Let cool completely, wrap tightly with freezer foil, and freeze. This can be kept frozen for up to 1 month.

To Prepare for Serving: Let meatballs and gravy thaw completely. Preheat oven to 350° F. Place wrapped container in oven and bake for 45 minutes. Unwrap, gently stir in rice, and serve.

BARCELONA BEEF AND RICE

Serves 4   **Approximately 8.7 g fat, 495 mg sodium per serving**

A colorful Spanish rice with beef, artichokes, black olives, and sweet red peppers.

Low-calorie cooking spray
¾ pound lean ground round
½ cup uncooked white rice
1 cup chopped yellow onion
1 16-ounce can chopped tomatoes,
　undrained
1½ cups water
½ teaspoon beef bouillon granules
1 cup slivered fresh green beans
¼ cup finely chopped red bell
　pepper
2 tablespoons chopped fresh
　parsley
¼ teaspoon garlic powder
¼ teaspoon turmeric
½ teaspoon paprika
¼ teaspoon black pepper
4 canned artichoke hearts,
　quartered
12 medium black olives, sliced

1. Coat a 10-inch nonstick skillet with a low-calorie cooking spray. Over medium-high heat, brown ground beef, about 3–4 minutes. Drain and discard excess grease. Place beef on paper towels to remove additional grease.

2. Return beef to skillet. Add rice, onion, tomatoes with liquid, water, bouillon granules, green beans, red pepper, parsley, garlic powder, turmeric, paprika, and black pepper. Bring to a boil, reduce heat, cover tightly, and simmer 25 minutes, or until beans are tender. Stir in artichoke hearts and olives. Cover and let stand 5 minutes before serving.

MAKE-AHEAD MEAL DIRECTIONS

To Freeze: Complete steps 1–2 of the recipe. Place mixture in an 8-inch square foil pan. Let cool completely, wrap tightly with freezer foil, and freeze. This can be kept frozen for up to 1 month.

To Prepare for Serving: Let mixture thaw completely. Preheat oven to 350° F. Place wrapped container in oven and bake for 50 minutes, stirring midway. Let stand 5 minutes before serving.

LEBANESE BEEF WITH EGGPLANT

Serves 4   **Approximately 9.7 g fat, 287 mg sodium per serving**

A sweetly spiced beef, eggplant, and noodle casserole, similar to a moussaka.

½ pound lean ground round
½ cup chopped yellow onion
1 garlic clove, minced
2 cups (about ½ pound) peeled
  and diced eggplant
1 cup chopped fresh tomato
1 tablespoon plus 2 teaspoons
  reduced-calorie, low-sodium
  catsup
1 tablespoon dry red wine
1 tablespoon dark brown sugar,
  packed
½ teaspoon plus ⅛ teaspoon apple
  pie spice
½ teaspoon dried oregano leaves
¼ teaspoon cinnamon
¼ teaspoon lemon zest
⅛ teaspoon nutmeg
1 cup cooked elbow macaroni
  (about 2 ounces dry) (no
  margarine or salt added during
  cooking)
1 egg
3 ounces "light" whipped cream
  cheese
½ cup (2 ounces) shredded
  reduced-calorie Swiss cheese
½ cup nonfat yogurt

1. Preheat oven to 350° F.
2. In a 10-inch ovenproof nonstick skillet, over medium-high heat, brown ground beef for about 3 minutes. Drain and discard excess grease. Place beef on paper towels to remove additional grease.
3. Return beef to skillet. Reduce heat to medium, add onion and garlic, and sauté 3–4 minutes. Add eggplant, tomatoes with liquid, catsup, wine, brown sugar, ½ teaspoon apple pie spice, oregano, cinnamon, lemon zest, and nutmeg. Mix thoroughly. Reduce heat, cover tightly, and simmer 25 minutes. Add macaroni and stir well.
4. In a food processor or blender, combine egg, cream cheese, Swiss cheese, and yogurt. Blend until smooth. Pour over meat mixture. Sprinkle with ⅛ teaspoon apple pie spice. Bake for 20–25 minutes.
5. Let stand 5–8 minutes. Slice into wedges and serve.

MAKE-AHEAD MEAL DIRECTIONS

To Freeze: Complete steps 1–3 of the recipe. Transfer mixture to an 8-inch square foil pan. Complete step 4. Let casserole cool completely, wrap tightly with freezer foil, and freeze. This can be kept frozen for up to 1 month.

To Prepare for Serving: Let mixture thaw completely. Preheat oven to 350° F. Place wrapped container in oven and bake for 35 minutes. Unwrap and bake 20 minutes longer. Let stand 5–8 minutes before serving.

❦ ❦

BLUE CHEESE BEEF AND NOODLE CASSEROLE

Serves 4

Approximately 7.3 g fat, 389 mg sodium per serving

Low-calorie cooking spray
½ pound lean ground round
1 garlic clove, minced
1½ cups skim milk
1 tablespoon flour
3 cups cooked egg noodles (about
   6 ounces dry) (no margarine or
   salt added during cooking)
2 tablespoons finely chopped
   green bell pepper
2 tablespoons chopped pimiento
⅜ teaspoon salt (if desired)
½ teaspoon freshly ground black
   pepper
2 tablespoons (1 ounce) crumbled
   blue cheese

1. Preheat oven to 350° F.

2. Coat a 10-inch ovenproof nonstick skillet with a low-calorie cooking spray. Over medium-high heat, brown ground beef and garlic for about 5–6 minutes. Drain and discard excess grease. Place beef on paper towels to remove additional grease. Wipe skillet dry with a paper towel.

3. Over medium heat, add milk to skillet and whisk in flour. Stir with a flat spatula until thickened, about 5–7 minutes. Remove from heat and add noodles, green pepper, pimiento, ¼ teaspoon salt, and black pepper. Add meat and blend well.

4. Top with blue cheese. Cover and bake for 13–15 minutes, or until heated thoroughly. Sprinkle with ⅛ teaspoon salt.

MAKE-AHEAD MEAL DIRECTIONS

To Freeze: Complete steps 2–3 of the recipe. Transfer mixture to an 8-inch square foil pan. Let casserole cool completely, wrap tightly with freezer foil, and freeze. This can be kept frozen for up to 1 month.

To Prepare for Serving: Let mixture thaw completely. Preheat oven to 350° F. Place wrapped container in oven and bake for 35 minutes. Unwrap and sprinkle with blue cheese. Cover with aluminum foil and bake 10 minutes longer. Sprinkle with ⅛ teaspoon salt.

QUICK VEGETABLE PARMESAN SOUP

Serves 4

Approximately 6.7 g fat, 498 mg sodium per serving

Low-calorie cooking spray
¾ pound lean ground round
1 garlic clove, minced
1 cup chopped yellow onion
2 cups coarsely chopped cabbage
1 10-ounce package frozen mixed
    vegetables
1 16-ounce can chopped tomatoes,
    undrained
2 tablespoons cider vinegar
1 teaspoon low-sodium
    Worcestershire sauce
¾ teaspoon sugar
1 bay leaf
¼ teaspoon salt (if desired)
⅛ teaspoon prepared hot sauce
¼ cup chopped fresh parsley
4 cups water
½ cup uncooked elbow macaroni
¼ cup grated Parmesan cheese

1. Coat a dutch oven, preferably cast-iron, with a low-calorie cooking spray. Over medium-high heat, brown ground beef for 4 minutes. Drain and discard excess grease. Place beef on paper towels to remove additional grease. Wipe dutch oven dry with a paper towel.

2. Return beef to dutch oven. Add garlic, onion, cabbage, mixed vegetables, tomatoes with liquid, vinegar, Worcestershire sauce, sugar, bay leaf, salt, hot sauce, parsley, and water. Bring to a boil, reduce heat, cover tightly, and simmer 12 minutes. Uncover, add macaroni, and simmer 15 more minutes. Remove bay leaf.

3. If possible, refrigerate soup overnight to improve flavors. Reheat soup and sprinkle each serving with 1 tablespoon Parmesan cheese.

MAKE-AHEAD MEAL DIRECTIONS

To Freeze: Complete steps 1–2 of the recipe. (Note: Do not continue to step 3.) Let soup cool completely. Place in two 1-gallon freezer bags. Seal bags tightly, allowing no excess air to remain, and freeze. This can be kept frozen for up to 1 month.

To Prepare for Serving: Let soup thaw completely. Pour into a dutch oven and cover tightly. Heat thoroughly over moderate heat, stirring occasionally. Sprinkle each serving with 1 tablespoon Parmesan cheese, if desired.

TORTILLA BAKE

Serves 4   **Approximately 9.8 g fat, 365 mg sodium per serving**

A flavorful, slightly spicy beef-and-sausage mixture, served with melted cheese, lettuce, tomatoes, and bell peppers.

Low-calorie cooking spray
¼ pound lean ground round
¼ pound hot or sweet Italian
    turkey sausage
½ cup chopped yellow onion
¼ cup chopped fresh parsley
½ teaspoon chili powder
½ teaspoon dried oregano leaves
¼ teaspoon cumin
4 10-inch flour tortillas
¼ cup plus 2 tablespoons (1½
    ounces) grated reduced-sodium,
    reduced-fat cheddar cheese
2 cups shredded lettuce
1½ cups chopped fresh tomato
¼ cup finely chopped green or red
    bell pepper
Freshly ground black pepper

1. Preheat oven to 425° F.
2. Coat a 10-inch nonstick skillet with a low-calorie cooking spray. Over medium-high heat, brown ground beef and sausage, stirring frequently, about 5 minutes. Drain and discard excess grease. Place beef on paper towels to remove additional grease. Wipe skillet dry with a paper towel.
3. Place onion in skillet and sauté until slightly browned, about 3 minutes. Add beef and sausage, parsley, chili powder, oregano, and cumin. Blend well.
4. Place tortillas on a foil-covered oven rack. Spoon meat mixture over entire flat tortillas. Top each with 1½ tablespoons cheese. Bake uncovered for 5–7 minutes, or until cheese melts.
5. Remove from oven and top with lettuce, tomato, bell pepper, and black pepper. Roll or serve open-faced.

MAKE-AHEAD MEAL DIRECTIONS

To Freeze: Complete steps 2–3 of the recipe. (Note: Do not continue to step 4.) Let meat mixture cool completely. Place in a 1-quart freezer bag. Seal bag tightly, allowing no excess air to remain, and freeze. This can be kept frozen for up to 1 month.

To Prepare for Serving: Let mixture thaw completely. Preheat oven to 425° F. Place tortillas on a foil-covered oven rack. Spoon meat mixture over entire flat tortillas. Top each with 3 tablespoons cheese. Bake uncovered for 10–12 minutes, or until cheese melts. Add toppings and serve as directed in step 5 of the recipe.

❖ ❖

SUPER SLOPPY JOES

Serves 4

Approximately 5.6 g fat, 457 mg sodium per serving

¾ pound lean ground round
1 medium yellow onion, chopped
 fine
½ green bell pepper, chopped fine
¼ teaspoon garlic powder
2 teaspoons chili powder
1 28-ounce can unsalted finely
 chopped tomatoes, drained
¼ cup chili sauce
¼ teaspoon beef bouillon granules
¼ cup water
1 teaspoon red wine vinegar
1 teaspoon dark brown sugar,
 packed
¾ teaspoon low-sodium
 Worcestershire sauce
¼ teaspoon salt (if desired)
4 reduced-calorie hamburger buns

1. In a 10-inch nonstick skillet, brown ground beef over medium heat. Drain and discard excess grease. Place beef on paper towels to remove additional grease. Wipe skillet dry with a paper towel.

2. Place onion, green pepper, and garlic powder in skillet and sauté 5 minutes. Add chili powder and blend well. Return the beef to the skillet and add tomatoes, chili sauce, beef bouillon granules, water, vinegar, sugar, Worcestershire sauce, and salt. Cook until vegetables are tender and sauce is thickened, about 20 minutes.

3. Divide mixture evenly over warmed buns.

Variation: In place of step 3, spoon beef mixture over 2 cups hot cooked macaroni instead of hamburger buns.

MAKE-AHEAD MEAL DIRECTIONS

To Freeze: Complete steps 1–2 of the recipe. (Note: Do not continue to step 3.) Let meat mixture cool completely. Place in a 1-quart freezer bag. Seal bag tightly, allowing no excess air to remain, and freeze. This can be kept frozen for up to 1 month.

To Prepare for Serving: Let mixture thaw completely. Pour into a medium saucepan. Heat thoroughly over moderate heat. Divide mixture evenly over warmed buns or spoon over hot cooked macaroni.

BAKED SKILLET PIZZA

Serves 4   **Approximately 9.7 g fat, 337 mg sodium per serving**

Ground beef, vegetables, tomato sauce, and Italian seasonings covered with a tender pie crust and melted mozzarella.

½ **pound lean ground round**
½ **green bell pepper, chopped**
½ **medium yellow onion, chopped**
1 **cup sliced fresh mushrooms**
1 **medium zucchini, sliced thin**
¼ **teaspoon garlic powder**
1 **medium tomato, chopped**
1 **teaspoon dried oregano leaves**
¼ **teaspoon salt (if desired)**
¼ **teaspoon red pepper flakes**
⅛ **teaspoon black pepper**
⅛ **teaspoon fennel seeds**
½ **cup flour**
1 **tablespoon vegetable oil**
1 **tablespoon plus 1 teaspoon**
   nonfat buttermilk
¾ **cup (3 ounces) shredded**
   mozzarella cheese

1. Preheat oven to 425° F.
2. In a 10-inch ovenproof nonstick skillet, brown ground beef over medium heat. Drain and discard excess grease. Place beef on paper towels to remove additional grease. Wipe skillet dry with a paper towel.
3. Place green pepper, onion, mushrooms, zucchini, and garlic powder in skillet. Cook over medium-high heat, stirring frequently, about 4–5 minutes or until vegetables are tender. Stir in tomato, oregano, salt, red pepper flakes, black pepper, fennel, and ground beef. Mix well.
4. In a small mixing bowl, combine flour, oil, and buttermilk. Blend well. Place on a fairly large sheet of plastic wrap, about 16 inches long. Top dough with another sheet of plastic wrap. Press down with rolling pin and roll dough out to make a thin pie crust. Place pie crust on top of mixture in skillet. Bake uncovered for 50–55 minutes, or until crust is golden brown.
5. Sprinkle with mozzarella. Let stand 20 minutes before serving.

MAKE-AHEAD MEAL DIRECTIONS

To Freeze: Complete steps 2–3 of the recipe. Prepare crust as directed in step 4. Let filling cool completely, then place pie crust on top. Do not bake. Wrap skillet tightly with freezer foil and freeze. This can be kept frozen for up to 1 month.

To Prepare for Serving: Do not thaw. Preheat oven to 425° F. Unwrap frozen pizza and bake for 1 hour, or until crust is golden brown. Sprinkle with mozzarella and Parmesan cheeses. Let stand 20 minutes before serving.

❦ ❦

THE QUARTER-POUND BURGER

Serves 4

Approximately 6.9 g fat, 416 mg sodium per serving

1 pound lean ground round
1 teaspoon barbecue smoke seasoning (I use Liquid Smoke)
2 garlic cloves, minced
Low-calorie cooking spray
¼ teaspoon freshly ground black pepper
4 reduced-calorie hamburger buns
¼ cup reduced-calorie, low-sodium catsup
4 teaspoons prepared mustard
½ medium yellow onion, cut into 4 slices
1 medium tomato, cut into 4 slices
4 lettuce leaves

1. Preheat broiler.

2. In a mixing bowl, combine ground beef, smoke seasoning, and garlic. Blend well and shape into four 4-inch patties.

3. Coat broiler rack with a low-calorie cooking spray. Place patties on rack and broil 2–3 inches away from heat source for 3 minutes. Turn, sprinkle with black pepper, and broil 2–3 minutes longer.

4. Run buns under broiler to toast, about 1 minute. Watch closely to be sure they do not burn. Place burgers on toasted buns. Add 1 tablespoon catsup, 1 teaspoon mustard, 1 slice each of onion and tomato, and a lettuce leaf.

MAKE-AHEAD MEAL DIRECTIONS

To Freeze: Prepare hamburger patties as directed in step 2 of the recipe. (Note: Do not continue to step 3.) Freeze in a single layer on a cookie sheet overnight. Transfer frozen patties to a 1-quart freezer bag. Seal bag tightly, allowing no excess air to remain, and freeze. This can be kept frozen for up to 2 months.

To Prepare for Serving: Do not thaw. Place frozen meat on a broiler rack coated with a low-calorie cooking spray. Broil 2–3 inches away from heat source for 4 minutes. Turn, sprinkle with black pepper, and broil 3–4 minutes longer. Toast buns and assemble burgers as directed in step 4 of the recipe.

ROQUEFORT-CHEDDAR BEEF

Serves 4   **Approximately 9.7 g fat, 303 mg sodium per serving**

Pan-fried ground round smothered with peppers, onions, and mushrooms, and topped with melted blue and cheddar cheeses.

1 pound lean ground round
1 tablespoon low-sodium
   Worcestershire sauce
1 tablespoon Dijon mustard
Low-calorie cooking spray
1 medium yellow onion, sliced in
   rings
1 medium green or red bell
   pepper, sliced in rings
½ pound fresh mushrooms,
   quartered
⅛ teaspoon salt (if desired)
¼ teaspoon garlic powder
¼ teaspoon black pepper
1 tablespoon dry red wine
1½ tablespoons (¾ ounce)
   crumbled blue cheese
¼ cup (1 ounce) grated low-
   sodium, reduced-fat cheddar
   cheese

1. In a mixing bowl, combine ground beef with Worcestershire sauce and Dijon mustard. Blend well and shape into 4 patties ¼ inch thick.

2. Coat a 10-inch nonstick skillet with a low-calorie cooking spray. Cook beef patties in the skillet over medium-high heat for 3 minutes. Flip patties and cook 2½–3 minutes longer. Drain and discard excess grease. Remove additional grease from beef patties by blotting them gently on each side with a paper towel. Wipe skillet dry with a paper towel.

3. Place onions, bell peppers, mushrooms, salt, garlic powder, and black pepper in skillet. Sauté until tender, about 8 minutes. Stir in wine and cook 1 minute longer. Reduce heat to very low and return beef patties to skillet. Spoon vegetables on top of patties. Top with blue and cheddar cheeses. Cover tightly and heat until cheeses melt, about 3–4 minutes. Serve immediately.

MAKE-AHEAD MEAL DIRECTIONS

To Freeze: Prepare hamburger patties as directed in step 1 of the recipe. (Note: Do not continue to step 2.) Freeze in a single layer on a cookie sheet overnight. Transfer frozen patties to a 1-quart freezer bag. Seal bag tightly, allowing no excess air to remain, and freeze. This can be kept frozen for up to 2 months.

To Prepare for Serving: Do not thaw. Complete steps 2–3 of the recipe, using frozen meat in step 2.

BEEF AND CORN MEXICANO

Serves 4

Approximately 9.1 g fat, 463 mg sodium per serving

Low-calorie cooking spray
¾ pound lean ground round
½ cup chopped yellow onion
1 16-ounce can chopped tomatoes, undrained
½ cup frozen corn kernels
1 small jalapeño pepper, minced (seeds discarded) *or* ⅛ teaspoon ground red pepper
1½ tablespoons chili powder
½ teaspoon dried oregano leaves
1 garlic clove, minced
½ teaspoon cumin
2 tablespoons chopped fresh parsley
¼ cup finely chopped green bell pepper
⅓ cup plus 1 tablespoon cornmeal
½ cup nonfat buttermilk
2 egg whites
½ teaspoon baking powder
¼ cup (1 ounce) grated Monterey Jack cheese with jalapeño peppers
¼ cup (1 ounce) grated low-sodium, reduced-fat cheddar cheese

1. Preheat oven to 350° F.
2. Coat a 10-inch ovenproof nonstick skillet with a low-calorie cooking spray. Over medium-high heat, brown ground beef about 4–5 minutes. Drain and discard excess grease. Place beef on paper towels to remove additional grease. Wipe skillet dry with a paper towel.
3. Sauté onion in skillet about 3 minutes over medium heat. Add tomatoes with liquid, corn, jalapeño pepper, chili powder, oregano, garlic, cumin, parsley, and ground beef. Reduce heat, cover tightly, and simmer 18–20 minutes. Stir in green pepper.
4. In a mixing bowl, combine cornmeal, buttermilk, egg whites, and baking powder. Blend well. Spoon over meat mixture and bake for 35 minutes, or until corn bread topping is done. Sprinkle with Monterey Jack and cheddar cheeses. Bake 5–7 minutes longer, or until cheese melts. Let stand 5 minutes before serving.

MAKE-AHEAD MEAL DIRECTIONS

To Freeze: Complete steps 2–3 of the recipe. (Note: Do not continue to step 4.) Place mixture in an 8-inch square foil pan. Let cool completely, wrap tightly with freezer foil, and freeze. This can be frozen for up to 1 month.

To Prepare for Serving: Let mixture thaw completely. Preheat oven to 350° F. In a mixing bowl, combine cornmeal, buttermilk, egg whites, and baking powder. Blend well. Spoon over meat mixture and bake for 45–50 minutes, or until corn bread topping is done.

Sprinkle with Monterey Jack and cheddar cheeses. Bake 5–7 minutes longer, or until cheese melts. Let stand 5 minutes before serving.

❧ ❧

MEXICAN BEEF AND RICE WITH SOUR CREAM

Serves 4   Approximately 7.3 g fat, 471 mg sodium per serving

A savory Mexican dish of beef, rice, and tomatoes spiced with chili powder and topped with sour cream and green onions.

¾ pound lean ground round
1 16-ounce can chopped unsalted
  tomatoes, undrained
⅔ cup prepared salsa
1 cup chopped yellow onion
2 tablespoons finely chopped
  green bell pepper
2 teaspoons chili powder
¼ teaspoon cumin
⅛ teaspoon garlic powder
¼ teaspoon turmeric
2 cups cooked rice (⅔ cup
  uncooked) (no margarine or salt
  added during cooking)
¼ cup nonfat plain yogurt
½ cup light sour cream
¼ cup chopped green onion

1. Preheat oven to 400° F.
2. In a 10-inch ovenproof nonstick skillet, brown ground beef over medium-high heat, about 6 minutes. Drain and discard excess grease. Place beef on paper towels to remove additional grease. Wipe skillet dry with a paper towel.
3. Return beef to skillet with tomatoes, salsa, onion, green pepper, chili powder, cumin, garlic powder, and turmeric. Reduce heat and simmer 10 minutes.
4. Stir in rice. Bake for 20 minutes. Remove from oven and let stand 5 minutes.
5. In a small bowl, combine yogurt and sour cream. Top each serving with 3 tablespoons of the sour cream mixture plus 1 tablespoon green onion.

MAKE-AHEAD MEAL DIRECTIONS

To Freeze: Complete steps 2–3 of the recipe. (Note: Do not continue to step 4.) Let mixture cool completely. Stir in rice and transfer mixture to an 8-inch square foil pan. Wrap tightly with freezer foil and freeze. This can be frozen for up to 1 month.

To Prepare for Serving: Let mixture thaw completely. Preheat oven to 350° F. Bake for 45–50 minutes, stirring occasionally. Remove from oven and let stand 5 minutes. Prepare and add toppings as directed in step 5 of the recipe.

6
✤ PORK ✤

Honey-Mustard Tenderloin
Creole Pork and Rice
Crumb-Coated Pork with Herbed Mustard
St. Thomas Tenderloin
Barbecued Pork Kabobs
Pork Tenders and Apples in Sweet Brandy Cream
Sweet and Sour Pork Stir-Fry
Roast Pork with Orange-Cranberry Relish
Garlic Tenderloin with Baked Apples
Herbed Pork Roast with Wild Rice
Lemon-Herbed Roast Pork with New Potatoes
Apricot-Glazed Pork with Baked Onions
Basil-Buttered Pork with Broccoli
Italian Pasta Salad
Pepperoni Pizzas
Mushroom-Bacon Crustless Tart
Stuffed Potatoes with Broccoli, Spicy Cheese Sauce, and Bacon
Creamy Bacon Pasta with Baked Tomato Halves
Jarlsberg Cauliflower

HONEY-MUSTARD TENDERLOIN

Serves 4   **Approximately 5.3 g fat, 296 mg sodium per serving**

Pork tenderloin with peppers and onions, slow-cooked in a curried honey-mustard sauce.

1½ tablespoons honey
⅓ cup Dijon mustard
2 tablespoons dark brown sugar, packed
⅛ teaspoon hot sauce
⅛ teaspoon curry powder
½ green *or* red bell pepper, thinly sliced
1 medium yellow onion, thinly sliced
¾ pound pork tenderloin, split lengthwise
2 cups hot cooked rice (no margarine or salt added during cooking)

1. In a 1-gallon freezer bag, combine honey, mustard, brown sugar, hot sauce, curry powder, bell pepper, and onion. Mix thoroughly and add pork. Seal bag, releasing any excess air. Shake to coat pork thoroughly. Marinate in refrigerator overnight, turning bag occasionally.

2. Preheat oven to 200° F.

3. Transfer meat and marinade from freezer bag to a 1½-quart casserole dish. Cover tightly and bake for 1½ hours. Increase heat to 325° F and bake 30 minutes longer. Let stand 5 minutes before slicing.

4. Arrange sliced meat in center of a serving platter. Spoon rice around meat. Pour sauce over all.

MAKE-AHEAD MEAL DIRECTIONS

To Freeze: Prepare marinade and coat vegetables and pork as directed in step 1 of the recipe. Freeze instead of marinating. (Note: Do not continue to step 2.) This can be kept frozen for up to 1 month.

To Prepare for Serving: Let mixture thaw completely, turning bag occasionally. Complete steps 2–4 of the recipe.

CREOLE PORK AND RICE

Serves 4

Approximately 8.4 g fat, 467 mg sodium per serving

Pork baked with bell peppers, tomatoes, okra, and rice, then topped with cheddar cheese.

Low-calorie cooking spray
¾ pound pork tenderloin, cut into bite-sized pieces
2 garlic cloves, minced
1 medium yellow onion, thinly sliced
½ cup thinly sliced green *or* red bell pepper
½ cup uncooked white rice
¾ teaspoon beef bouillon granules
⅛ teaspoon freshly ground black pepper
1 16-ounce can chopped tomatoes, undrained
⅓ cup water
12 fresh whole okra, tops removed
⅛ teaspoon ground red pepper
⅔ cup (2½ ounces) grated low-sodium, reduced-fat sharp cheddar cheese

1. Preheat oven to 350° F.
2. Coat a 10-inch ovenproof nonstick skillet with a low-calorie cooking spray. Brown pork and garlic over high heat for about 3–5 minutes. Drain and discard excess grease. Place pork on paper towels to remove additional grease. Wipe skillet dry with a paper towel.
3. Coat the same skillet with a low-calorie cooking spray. Over medium-high heat, sauté onion about 2–3 minutes. Remove from heat and add bell pepper, rice, beef bouillon granules, black pepper, tomatoes with liquid, water, okra, red pepper, and pork. Stir well.
4. Cover tightly and bake for 50–60 minutes, or until rice is done. Top with cheese and bake uncovered 5–6 minutes longer. Let stand 5–6 minutes before serving.

MAKE-AHEAD MEAL DIRECTIONS

To Freeze: Complete steps 2–3 of the recipe. (Note: Do not continue to step 4.) Place mixture in an 8-inch square foil pan. Let cool completely, wrap tightly with freezer foil, and freeze. This can be kept frozen for up to 1 month.

To Prepare for Serving: Let mixture thaw completely. Preheat oven to 350° F. Place wrapped container in oven and bake for about 1 hour, or until rice is done. Unwrap, top with cheese, and bake 8–10 minutes longer. Let stand 5–6 minutes before serving.

CRUMB-COATED PORK WITH HERBED MUSTARD

Serves 4

Approximately 8.4 g fat, 495 mg sodium per serving

¼ cup plus 1 tablespoon Dijon
  mustard
½ teaspoon dried sage leaves
¼ teaspoon dried rosemary leaves
¼ teaspoon dried thyme leaves
2 tablespoons extra-virgin olive oil
1 pound pork tenderloin, cut into
  1-inch pieces
4 slices reduced-calorie bread,
  toasted and grated
Low-calorie cooking spray
4 medium zucchini, halved
  lengthwise
2 teaspoons fresh lemon juice
½ teaspoon lemon pepper

1. In a 1-quart freezer bag, combine mustard, sage, rosemary, thyme, and 2 tablespoons olive oil. Mix thoroughly and add pork. Seal bag, releasing any excess air. Shake to coat pork thoroughly. Marinate in refrigerator overnight or at least 2 hours.

2. Preheat the broiler.

3. Remove pork from bag, discarding marinade. Roll pork in bread crumbs and place in a single layer on a broiler pan coated with a low-calorie cooking spray. Arrange zucchini halves around pork pieces. Spoon ¼ teaspoon lemon juice onto each half. Sprinkle lemon pepper over zucchini.

4. Broil at least 5 inches away from heat source for 3 minutes. Turn pork and broil 2½ minutes longer. Arrange pork and zucchini on a serving platter and serve immediately.

MAKE-AHEAD MEAL DIRECTIONS

To Freeze: Prepare marinade and coat pork as directed in step 1 of the recipe. Freeze instead of marinating. (Note: Do not continue to step 2.) This can be kept frozen for up to 1 month.

To Prepare for Serving: Let mixture thaw completely. Shake to coat pork evenly. Complete steps 2–4 of the recipe.

ST. THOMAS TENDERLOIN

Serves 4   **Approximately 9.8 g fat, 119 mg sodium per serving**

A delectable blend of pineapple, pork, and peppers, flavored with just a hint of rum and served with sweet potatoes.

¾ cup water
¾ pound peeled sweet potato,
    sliced ¼ inch thick
Low-calorie cooking spray
¾ pound pork tenderloin, cut into
    thin strips
1½ cups thinly sliced yellow onion
¾ cup unsweetened pineapple
    tidbits with juice
2 tablespoons fresh lime juice
1 tablespoon dark brown sugar,
    packed
½ teaspoon curry powder
¼ teaspoon cinnamon
⅛ teaspoon salt (if desired)
⅛ teaspoon ground red pepper
2 tablespoons rum
2 teaspoons cornstarch
¼ cup chopped pecans, toasted
    under broiler

1. Bring water to a boil in a 10-inch ovenproof nonstick skillet. Add sweet potato, reduce heat, cover tightly, and simmer 5 minutes. Drain well, remove from skillet, and set aside. Cover and keep warm.

2. Coat skillet with a low-calorie cooking spray and heat over high heat. Add pork and brown about 3 minutes. Using a slotted spoon, remove pork from skillet and set aside.

3. Add onion to any remaining drippings. Stir-fry over medium-high heat for about 5 minutes. Return pork to skillet, along with pineapple and its juice, lime juice, brown sugar, curry, cinnamon, salt, and red pepper. Reduce heat, cover, and simmer 12–15 minutes, or until pork is tender.

4. In a small glass, combine rum and cornstarch, and mix well. Add cornstarch mixture and pecans to skillet. Increase heat to medium-high, stirring constantly, until sauce is slightly thickened, about 3 minutes.

5. Spoon pork and pineapple mixture onto a serving platter. Arrange sweet potatoes around pork and pineapple. Serve immediately.

Do Not Freeze

BARBECUED PORK KABOBS

Serves 4   **Approximately 9.8 g fat, 450 mg sodium per serving**

Skewered pork, bacon, and vegetables in a hickory-smoked glaze.

2 8-ounce baking potatoes
⅓ cup barbecue sauce
2 tablespoons dry red wine
¾ pound pork tenderloin, cut into bite-sized pieces
4 slices "lower-salt" bacon, cut into eighths (32 pieces)
1 medium yellow onion, cut into eighths, layers separated
½ cup (4 ounces) halved water chestnuts
1 large green bell pepper, cut into 1-inch pieces
1 tablespoon plus 1 teaspoon low-calorie margarine
2 tablespoons chopped green onion
Freshly ground black pepper

1. Preheat oven to 350° F.
2. Wrap potatoes individually in aluminum foil. Bake 1 hour. Remove from oven and set aside. In a small mixing bowl, combine barbecue sauce and wine and set aside.
3. Preheat broiler.
4. Thread pork, bacon, onion, water chestnuts, and bell pepper alternately onto eight 12-inch skewers. Broil 2–3 inches away from heat source for 4–5 minutes. Turn and broil 2 more minutes. Spoon sauce over meat only and broil 2–3 minutes longer.
5. Split potatoes in half lengthwise. Spread 1 teaspoon margarine on each half. Sprinkle with green onion and black pepper.

Do Not Freeze

PORK TENDERS AND APPLES IN SWEET BRANDY CREAM

Serves 4   **Approximately 8.8 g fat, 250 mg sodium per serving**

Lightly fried tenderloin medallions and onions, cooked with apples and brandy and served with broccoli.

1 cup water
4 cups fresh broccoli flowerets
¾ pound pork tenderloin, thinly sliced into medallions
2 tablespoons flour
¼ teaspoon salt
⅛ teaspoon freshly ground black pepper
Low-calorie cooking spray
2 teaspoons vegetable oil
2 garlic cloves, minced
1½ cups thinly sliced yellow onion
1 medium apple, peeled and thinly sliced
2 tablespoons brandy
⅓ cup unsalted canned condensed chicken broth, undiluted
½ cup evaporated skim milk
Lemon wedges (if desired)

1. Bring water to a boil in a 10-inch nonstick skillet. Add broccoli, reduce heat, cover tightly, and simmer for 4 minutes or until tender but still crisp. Drain and remove from skillet. Set aside and keep warm.

2. Sift flour over both sides of pork medallions. Sprinkle with salt and pepper. Coat skillet with a low-calorie cooking spray. Heat oil and garlic over medium-high heat. When bubbly, add pork and cook 3 minutes. Turn and cook 3 minutes longer. Remove from skillet.

3. In any remaining pan drippings, sauté onion 3 minutes. Add apple slices and cook 2–3 minutes longer. Add pork, brandy, and chicken broth. Reduce heat and simmer uncovered for 3–4 minutes. Add evaporated milk, increase heat to medium, and cook 3 minutes longer, or until sauce is slightly thickened.

4. Place pork mixture in center of a serving platter. Arrange broccoli around pork. Serve with lemon wedges for broccoli, if desired.

Do Not Freeze

❧ ❧

SWEET AND SOUR PORK STIR-FRY

Serves 4

Approximately 9.1 g fat, 348 mg sodium per serving

2 tablespoons dark brown sugar, packed

2 tablespoons low-sodium soy sauce

2 tablespoons cider vinegar

1 tablespoon cornstarch

2 tablespoons water

2 tablespoons flour

¾ pound pork tenderloin, thinly sliced into medallions

Low-calorie cooking spray

1 tablespoon plus 2 teaspoons vegetable oil

2 medium green bell peppers, cut into bite-sized pieces

1 medium-sized yellow onion, cut into eighths and layers separated

1 medium carrot, peeled and cut into matchsticks

1 8-ounce can pineapple tidbits in juice, undrained

1. In a small mixing bowl, combine brown sugar, soy sauce, vinegar, cornstarch, and water. Blend thoroughly and set aside.

2. Sift flour over both sides of pork medallions. Coat a 10-inch nonstick skillet with a low-calorie cooking spray. Add 1 tablespoon oil and heat for 1 minute over medium-high heat. Add pork and sauté for 3 minutes. Turn and cook 2–3 minutes longer. Place on serving platter.

3. Add remaining 2 teaspoons oil to skillet. Add green peppers, onion, and carrot. Stir-fry 4 minutes, or until vegetables are tender but still crisp. Stir in soy sauce mixture and pineapple tidbits with liquid. Bring to a boil and cook 1–2 minutes longer, or until sauce is thickened. Stir in pork and cook 1 minute longer. Serve immediately.

Do Not Freeze

ROAST PORK WITH ORANGE-CRANBERRY RELISH

Serves 4

Approximately 7.4 g fat, 246 mg sodium per serving

1 cup finely chopped fresh or
    frozen cranberries
¼ cup orange juice concentrate
½ teaspoon orange zest
2 tablespoons plus 2 teaspoons
    sugar
1 pound pork tenderloin
⅛ teaspoon garlic powder
¼ teaspoon dried sage leaves
¼ teaspoon dried thyme leaves
¼ teaspoon salt (if desired)
¼ teaspoon black pepper
2 cups hot cooked rice (no salt or
    margarine added during
    cooking)
1 teaspoon butter substitute (I use
    Molly McButter)
1 tablespoon chopped fresh
    parsley

1. Preheat oven to 325° F.
2. In a 1-pint freezer bag, combine cranberries, orange juice concentrate, orange zest, and sugar. Mix thoroughly. Seal bag, releasing any excess air. Set aside.
3. Sprinkle pork with garlic powder, sage, thyme, salt, and black pepper. Place on a baking rack and bake 55–60 minutes. Let stand 6–8 minutes, then slice thin.
4. Place cranberry relish in center of a large serving platter. Arrange pork slices around relish. Toss hot rice with butter substitute and arrange around outer edges of pork. Sprinkle with parsley and serve immediately.

Variation: The cranberry relish may be served frozen after being shaved with a fork. (See freezing instructions under Make-Ahead Meal Directions.) This makes a refreshing ice. Serve in a separate bowl.

MAKE-AHEAD MEAL DIRECTIONS

To Freeze: Prepare cranberry relish as directed in step 2 of the recipe. Freeze. (Note: Do not continue to step 3.)

Sprinkle pork with garlic powder, sage, thyme, salt, and black pepper. Place pork in a 1-gallon freezer bag. Seal bag tightly, allowing no excess air to remain, and freeze.

Pork and cranberries can be kept frozen for up to 1 month.

To Prepare for Serving: Let pork and cranberry relish thaw completely. Preheat oven to 325° F. Place pork on a baking rack and bake 55–60 minutes. Let stand 6–8 minutes, then slice thin. Serve as directed in step 4 of the recipe.

GARLIC TENDERLOIN WITH BAKED APPLES

Serves 4

Approximately 9.6 g fat, 233 mg sodium per serving

1 pound pork tenderloin
1 teaspoon cracked black pepper
5 garlic cloves, minced
2 tablespoons finely chopped fresh
  parsley
¼ teaspoon salt (if desired)
4 medium Red Delicious apples,
  halved
3 tablespoons pecans, toasted
  under broiler
1 tablespoon dark brown sugar,
  packed
1 tablespoon plus 1 teaspoon low-
  calorie margarine
½ teaspoon vanilla extract
¼ teaspoon cinnamon
⅛ teaspoon nutmeg
Low-calorie cooking spray

1. Thoroughly coat pork with pepper, garlic, parsley, and salt. Marinate in refrigerator at least 2 hours.

2. Preheat oven to 325° F.

3. Carefully cut out core of each apple half, forming a well in the center. In a small mixing bowl, combine pecans, brown sugar, margarine, vanilla, cinnamon, and nutmeg. Blend well. Place equal amounts in each apple half. Place apple halves and pork on a broiler rack coated with a low-calorie cooking spray.

4. Bake for 45 minutes. Remove apples and cook pork 10–15 minutes longer. Let pork stand 6–8 minutes before slicing.

MAKE-AHEAD MEAL DIRECTIONS

To Freeze: Season pork as directed in step 1 of the recipe. (Note: Do not continue to step 2.) Instead of marinating, place pork in a 1-gallon freezer bag. Seal bag tightly, allowing no excess air to remain, and freeze. This can be kept frozen for up to 1 month.

To Prepare for Serving: Let pork thaw completely. Complete steps 2–4 of the recipe.

HERBED PORK ROAST WITH WILD RICE

Serves 4

Approximately 10.0 g fat, 250 mg sodium per serving

2 tablespoons fresh lime juice
1 tablespoon low-sodium soy sauce
1 tablespoon vegetable oil
½ teaspoon black pepper
½ teaspoon freshly grated ginger
   root
¼ teaspoon dried thyme leaves
¼ teaspoon dried sage leaves
1 pound pork tenderloin
Low-calorie cooking spray
2 cups hot cooked wild rice (no
   margarine or salt added during
   cooking)
2 tablespoons chopped pimiento
3 tablespoons chopped fresh
   parsley

1. In a 1-quart freezer bag, combine lime juice, soy sauce, oil, black pepper, ginger, thyme, and sage. Mix thoroughly and add pork. Seal bag, releasing any excess air. Shake to coat pork thoroughly. Marinate in refrigerator overnight or at least 2 hours.

2. Preheat oven to 325° F.

3. Place pork on a broiler rack coated with a low-calorie cooking spray. Pour any remaining marinade over pork. Bake 55–60 minutes. Let stand 6–8 minutes, then slice thin.

4. Place hot rice in center of a serving platter and toss with pimiento and 2 tablespoons parsley. Arrange pork slices around rice. Sprinkle pork with remaining 1 tablespoon parsley.

MAKE-AHEAD MEAL DIRECTIONS

To Freeze: Prepare marinade and coat pork as directed in step 1 of the recipe. Freeze instead of marinating. (Note: Do not continue to step 2.) This can be kept frozen for up to 1 month.

To Prepare for Serving: Let pork thaw completely. Shake to coat pork evenly. Complete steps 2–4 of the recipe.

LEMON-HERBED ROAST PORK WITH NEW POTATOES

Serves 4

Approximately 9.1 g fat, 351 mg sodium per serving

1 whole lemon
1½ tablespoons extra-virgin olive oil
3 garlic cloves, minced
½ teaspoon dry mustard
½ teaspoon salt (if desired)
½ teaspoon freshly ground black pepper
½ teaspoon dried rosemary leaves
¼ teaspoon dried thyme leaves
¼ cup chopped fresh parsley
1 pound pork tenderloin
Low-calorie cooking spray
12 small new potatoes (about 1 ounce each)
Paprika

1. Squeeze juice from lemon and grate peel. In a mixing bowl, combine juice and zest with olive oil, garlic, mustard, ¼ teaspoon salt, pepper, rosemary, thyme, and parsley. Mix well. Place pork in a 1-gallon freezer bag. Pour marinade over pork and seal bag tightly, releasing any excess air. Shake to coat pork thoroughly. Marinate in refrigerator at least 6 hours.

2. Preheat oven to 325° F.

3. Remove pork from freezer bag, reserving marinade, and place on a baking rack coated with a low-calorie cooking spray.

4. Peel a ¼-inch-wide strip of skin from around each potato. Toss potatoes in remaining marinade and arrange around pork. Drizzle marinade over pork; sprinkle with paprika and remaining ¼ teaspoon salt. Bake uncovered for 55–60 minutes. Let pork stand 6–8 minutes, then slice thin.

MAKE-AHEAD MEAL DIRECTIONS

To Freeze: Prepare marinade and coat pork as directed in step 1 of the recipe. Freeze instead of marinating. (Note: Do not continue to step 2.) This can be kept frozen for up to 1 month.

To Prepare for Serving: Let pork thaw completely. Shake to coat pork evenly. Complete steps 2–4 of the recipe.

APRICOT-GLAZED PORK WITH BAKED ONIONS

Serves 4

Approximately 7.7 g fat, 292 mg sodium per serving

1 pound pork tenderloin
2 teaspoons Dijon mustard
1 teaspoon orange juice
   concentrate
1½ teaspoons dark brown sugar,
   packed
½ teaspoon orange zest
½ teaspoon ground ginger
⅛ teaspoon garlic powder
4 medium yellow onions, halved
2 tablespoons plus 2 teaspoons
   low-sodium soy sauce
Freshly ground black pepper, to
   taste
¼ cup apricot jam

1. Unfold pork tenderloin. Brush center with mustard and orange juice concentrate. Sprinkle with brown sugar, orange zest, ginger, and garlic powder. Fold pork and secure with ties or toothpicks. Place in a 1-gallon freezer bag. Seal tightly, releasing as much air as possible. Marinate in refrigerator overnight or at least 2 hours.

2. Preheat oven to 325° F.

3. Wrap onion halves individually with aluminum foil, leaving top open. Spoon ½ teaspoon soy sauce on each half, and top with black pepper. Place pork on a baking rack coated with a low-calorie cooking spray and sprinkle with black pepper. Arrange foil-wrapped onions around pork and bake for 30 minutes. Spoon jam over top of pork and continue baking for 20–25 minutes.

4. Remove pork from oven, let stand 6–8 minutes, and slice. Spoon remaining soy sauce on onions at time of serving.

MAKE-AHEAD MEAL DIRECTIONS

To Freeze: Prepare marinade and coat pork as directed in step 1 of the recipe. Freeze instead of marinating. (Note: Do not continue to step 2.) This can be kept frozen for up to 1 month.

To Prepare for Serving: Let pork thaw completely. Complete steps 2–4 of the recipe.

BASIL-BUTTERED PORK WITH BROCCOLI

Serves 4

Approximately 9.5 g fat, 285 mg sodium per serving

2 tablespoons low-calorie
   margarine
1 tablespoon fresh lemon juice
½ green onion, minced
2 garlic cloves, minced
¼ teaspoon salt (if desired)
1 teaspoon dried basil leaves
½ teaspoon dried dill weed
4 3-ounce lean boneless center cut
   pork loin chops
¾ cup plus ⅓ cup water
½ teaspoon chicken bouillon
   granules
3 cups fresh broccoli flowerets
Low-calorie cooking spray
Lemon wedges

1. In a small mixing bowl, combine margarine, lemon juice, green onion, garlic, salt, basil, and dill. Blend well. Coat both sides of pork chops completely with herb-butter mixture. Wrap in plastic wrap and marinate in the refrigerator overnight or at least 2 hours.

2. In a 10-inch nonstick skillet, combine ¾ cup water and chicken bouillon granules. Bring to boil and add broccoli. Cover tightly, reduce heat, and simmer 3–4 minutes, or until broccoli is tender but still crisp. Drain broccoli and arrange around outside of a serving platter. Cover and keep warm. Wipe skillet dry with a paper towel.

3. Coat skillet with a low-calorie cooking spray. Heat 1 minute over medium-high heat. Add pork chops and sauté for 3 minutes. Turn and cook 2½–3 minutes more, or until done. Place pork chops in center of the serving platter.

4. Pour the remaining ⅓ cup water in skillet and boil 1 minute, scraping bottom and sides of skillet. Pour sauce over meat. Serve immediately with lemon wedges.

MAKE-AHEAD MEAL DIRECTIONS

To Freeze: Prepare marinade and coat pork as directed in step 1 of the recipe. Wrap chops individually in freezer plastic wrap. Freeze instead of marinating. (Note: Do not continue to step 2.) This can be kept frozen for up to 1 month.

To Prepare for Serving: Let pork thaw completely. Complete steps 2–4 of the recipe.

ITALIAN PASTA SALAD

Serves 4   **Approximately 9.9 g fat, 462 mg sodium per serving**

A colorful pasta salad with salami, artichoke hearts, tomatoes, olives, and more.

¼ cup fresh lemon juice
2 tablespoons extra-virgin olive oil
½ teaspoon dry mustard
½ teaspoon dried oregano leaves
¼ teaspoon dried basil leaves
¼ teaspoon garlic powder
¼ teaspoon salt (if desired)
¼ teaspoon black pepper
3½ cups hot cooked and cooled
   multicolored corkscrew or shell
   pasta (no salt added during
   cooking)
4 canned artichoke hearts,
   quartered
2 tablespoons finely chopped
   yellow onion
2 tablespoons finely chopped
   green bell pepper
8 medium black olives, thinly
   sliced
1 cup fresh tender spinach leaves
2 cups ⅛-inch crosswise slices ripe
   plum tomato
2 slices hard salami
Freshly cracked black pepper

1. In a 1-gallon freezer bag, combine lemon juice, olive oil, dry mustard, oregano, basil, garlic powder, salt, and black pepper. Mix thoroughly. Add pasta, artichoke hearts, onion, green pepper, and olives. Toss well to coat thoroughly. Seal bag, releasing any excess air. Marinate in the refrigerator overnight or at least 2 hours.

2. On individual dinner plates, arrange spinach leaves around half of plate and tomato slices around other side. Cut salami into extremely thin strips and sprinkle over spinach. Sprinkle all with cracked pepper (if desired).

3. Toss pasta mixture again. Spoon ¼ of the mixture onto the center of each plate. Serve immediately.

MAKE-AHEAD MEAL DIRECTIONS

To Freeze: Prepare dressing and coat pasta and vegetables as directed in step 1 of the recipe. Freeze instead of marinating. (Note: Do not continue to step 2.) This can be kept frozen for up to 2 weeks.

To Prepare for Serving: On the day of serving, let vegetable mixture thaw completely. Toss mixture thoroughly in bag. Complete steps 2–3 of the recipe.

PEPPERONI PIZZAS

Serves 4

Approximately 9.6 g fat, 414 mg sodium per serving

4 6-inch flour tortillas
¾ cup no-salt tomato sauce
½ teaspoon dried oregano leaves
¼ teaspoon fennel seeds
⅛ teaspoon garlic powder
⅛ teaspoon salt (if desired)
⅛ teaspoon freshly ground black
  pepper
½ teaspoon red pepper flakes
1½ ounces (28 slices) pepperoni
¾ cup (3 ounces) shredded
  mozzarella cheese

1. Preheat oven to 475° F.
2. Place tortillas on a foil-lined oven rack. Heat in oven for 2 minutes. Remove from oven and reduce heat to 350° F.
3. Cover each tortilla with equal amounts of tomato sauce, oregano, fennel, garlic powder, salt, black pepper, red pepper flakes, pepperoni, and mozzarella.
4. Bake for 5–7 minutes and serve.

MAKE-AHEAD MEAL DIRECTIONS

To Freeze: Complete steps 1–3 of the recipe. (Note: Do not continue to step 4.) Let pizzas cool completely. Place each in a 1-quart freezer bag. Seal each bag tightly, allowing no excess air to remain, and freeze. This can be kept frozen for up to 1 month.

To Prepare for Serving: Do not thaw. Preheat oven to 350° F. Remove frozen pizzas from bags and place on a foil-lined oven rack. Bake for 5–7 minutes. Top each pizza with 2 teaspoons Parmesan cheese.

MUSHROOM-BACON CRUSTLESS TART

Serves 4

Approximately 9.8 g fat, 262 mg sodium per serving

4 slices ''lower-salt'' bacon
2 cups sliced fresh mushrooms
1 green onion, chopped
Low-calorie cooking spray
1 large egg
3 large egg whites
⅓ cup evaporated skim milk
1 tablespoon Dijon mustard
⅛ teaspoon nutmeg
⅛–¼ teaspoon black pepper, to taste
½ cup plus 2 tablespoons (2½ ounces) grated Lorraine Swiss cheese

1. Preheat oven to 350° F.
2. In a 10-inch nonstick skillet, cook bacon over medium-high heat until crisp. Drain and discard excess grease. Place bacon on paper towels and blot to remove additional grease. Crumble bacon. Wipe skillet dry with a paper towel.
3. In the same skillet, sauté mushrooms and onion over medium heat for about 5 minutes or until tender. Remove from skillet and drain on paper towels.
4. In a 9-inch pie pan coated with a low-calorie cooking spray, combine egg, egg whites, evaporated milk, mustard, nutmeg, and black pepper. Blend well. Stir in cheese, mushrooms, and onions, and mix well. Sprinkle crumbled bacon on top and bake for 25 minutes. Let stand 5 minutes before serving.

MAKE-AHEAD MEAL DIRECTIONS

To Freeze: Complete steps 1–4 of the recipe. Let tart cool completely. Wrap tightly with freezer foil and freeze. This can be kept frozen for up to 2 weeks.

To Prepare for Serving: Let tart thaw completely. Preheat oven to 350° F. Unwrap tart and bake for 20 minutes. Let stand 5 minutes before serving.

STUFFED POTATOES WITH BROCCOLI, SPICY CHEESE SAUCE, AND BACON

Serves 4

Approximately 3.4 g fat, 427 mg sodium per serving

4 8-ounce baking potatoes
4 slices "lower-salt" bacon
¾ cup water
3 cups fresh broccoli flowerets
1¼ cups skim milk
1 tablespoon cornstarch
Dash ground red pepper
½ cup (2 ounces) grated reduced-fat cheddar cheese
2 tablespoons chopped pimiento
¼ teaspoon salt

1. Preheat oven to 350° F.
2. Wrap potatoes individually in aluminum foil. Bake for 1 hour.
3. While potatoes are baking, fry bacon in a 10-inch nonstick skillet over medium-high heat until crisp. Drain and discard excess grease. Place bacon on paper towels and blot well to remove additional grease. Wipe skillet dry with a paper towel.
4. In the same skillet, bring water to a boil. Add broccoli, reduce heat, cover tightly, and simmer about 4 minutes, or until broccoli is tender but still crisp. Drain broccoli, remove from skillet, and set aside.
5. In a mixing bowl, combine milk and cornstarch. Blend well and pour into skillet. Over medium-high heat, stirring with a flat spatula, bring mixture to a boil and cook 2–3 minutes, or until thickened. Remove from heat and add ground red pepper, cheese, and pimiento. Stir until cheese melts.
6. Split potatoes and fluff gently with a fork, being careful not to tear outer skin. Place an equal amount of broccoli on each of the potatoes. Pour sauce over each, and top with 1 slice of bacon, crumbled.

Do Not Freeze

CREAMY BACON PASTA WITH BAKED TOMATO HALVES

Serves 4   Approximately 7.0 g fat, 422 mg sodium per serving

Freshly cooked egg noodles tossed with bacon in a light cheese and cream sauce, served with baked tomatoes and Parmesan.

4 slices "lower-salt" bacon
4 cups cooked medium egg noodles (about 8 ounces dry) (no margarine or salt added during cooking)
¼ cup skim milk
¼ cup evaporated skim milk
¼ cup (1 ounce) shredded mozzarella cheese *or* grated reduced-fat Swiss cheese
¼ teaspoon freshly ground black pepper
⅛ teaspoon garlic powder
⅜ teaspoon salt (if desired)
2 tablespoons plus 2 teaspoons grated Parmesan cheese
2 medium tomatoes, halved

1. Preheat oven to 325° F.

2. In a 10-inch ovenproof nonstick skillet, fry bacon over medium-high heat until very crisp. Drain and discard excess grease. Place bacon on paper towels and blot well to remove additional grease. Crumble bacon. Wipe skillet dry with a paper towel.

3. In the same skillet, combine bacon, noodles, skim milk, evaporated milk, mozzarella or Swiss cheese, black pepper, garlic powder, ¼ teaspoon salt, and 1 tablespoon Parmesan cheese. Toss well.

4. Place tomato halves on a foil-lined oven rack. Sprinkle ⅛ teaspoon salt over tomato halves. Sprinkle each with ½ teaspoon Parmesan cheese. Bake tomato halves and uncovered pasta for 25–30 minutes. Top pasta with the remaining 1 tablespoon of Parmesan cheese.

Do Not Freeze

JARLSBERG CAULIFLOWER

Serves 4   **Approximately 9.9 g fat, 398 mg sodium per serving**

Swiss cheese and cauliflower crowned with bacon and green onions.

Low-calorie cooking spray
4 slices "lower-salt" bacon
¾ cup water
4 cups cauliflower flowerets
¾ cup (3 ounces) grated Jarlsberg
  Swiss cheese
¼ cup chopped green onion
⅓ cup evaporated skim milk
⅓ cup plus 1 tablespoon skim milk
2 eggs plus 3 egg whites
1 jalapeño pepper, seeded and
  finely chopped
1 garlic clove, minced
¼ teaspoon salt (if desired)
⅛ teaspoon black pepper

1. Preheat oven to 325° F.

2. Coat a 10-inch ovenproof nonstick skillet with a low-calorie cooking spray. Over medium-high heat, fry bacon until very crisp. Drain and discard excess grease. Place bacon on paper towels and blot well to remove additional grease. Wipe skillet dry with a paper towel.

3. In the same skillet, bring water to a boil. Add cauliflower, reduce heat, cover tightly, and simmer 5 minutes, or until tender. Drain well, remove cauliflower from skillet, and set aside.

4. Recoat skillet with low-calorie cooking spray. Place ½ cup cheese on bottom of skillet. Add cauliflower. In a mixing bowl, place green onions, evaporated milk, skim milk, eggs and egg whites, jalapeño pepper, garlic, salt, and black pepper. Mix well and pour over cauliflower and cheese. Top with remaining cheese and sprinkle with crumbled bacon. Bake for 35–45 minutes, or until done in center. Let stand 10 minutes before serving.

Do Not Freeze

7
✦ MEATLESS ✦

Asparagus-Cheddar Tart
Pesto Pasta
Chili-Cheese Tart
Spinach and Cheese–Stuffed Pasta Shells
Three-Cheese Ziti
Cheesy Vegetable-Stuffed Potatoes
Zucchini Lasagna
Tortilla Pizza
Cheddar-Onion Potato "Skins" with Sour Cream
The Sophisticated Scramble
Veggie-Stuffed Pitas
Pasta Salad with Tomatoes and Feta
Taco Salad Supreme
The Classic Main Salad
Summer Days Fruit Salad

ASPARAGUS-CHEDDAR TART

Serves 4

Approximately 9.3 g fat, 251 mg sodium per serving

⅓ cup water
3 cups 2-inch-long pieces fresh
    asparagus
Low-calorie cooking spray
2 large eggs
2 large egg whites
⅓ cup evaporated skim milk
1 tablespoon Dijon mustard
⅛ teaspoon nutmeg
⅛ teaspoon black pepper
½ cup plus 2 tablespoons (2½
    ounces) grated New York extra-
    sharp cheddar cheese

1. Preheat oven to 350° F.

2. In a 10-inch skillet, bring water to a boil and add asparagus. Reduce heat, cover tightly, and simmer 3–4 minutes, or until asparagus is just tender but still crisp. Drain well.

3. Coat a 9-inch pie pan with a low-calorie cooking spray. Combine eggs and egg whites, evaporated milk, mustard, nutmeg, and black pepper in a pie pan and blend well. Stir in cheese and asparagus. Mix well.

4. Bake for 25 minutes. Let stand 5 minutes before serving.

MAKE-AHEAD MEAL DIRECTIONS

To Freeze: Complete steps 1–3 of the recipe. (Note: Do not continue to step 4.) Bake tart for 25 minutes. Let cool completely, wrap tightly with freezer foil, and freeze. This can be kept frozen for up to 2 weeks.

To Prepare for Serving: Let tart thaw completely. Preheat oven to 350° F. Unwrap tart and bake for 20 minutes. Let stand 5 minutes before serving.

PESTO PASTA

Serves 4

Approximately 9.6 g fat, 496 mg sodium per serving

¾ cup firmly packed fresh spinach
   leaves
2 tablespoons extra-virgin olive oil
2 tablespoons grated Parmesan
   cheese
2 garlic cloves, minced
2 tablespoons chopped fresh
   parsley
1 teaspoon dried basil leaves
1 tablespoon sesame seeds
¾ teaspoon salt
⅛ teaspoon freshly ground black
   pepper
2 tablespoons chopped yellow
   onion
1½ tablespoons fresh lemon juice
5 cups hot cooked spaghetti (no
   salt added during cooking)

1. In a food processor or blender, combine spinach, olive oil, 1 tablespoon Parmesan cheese, garlic, parsley, basil, sesame seeds, salt, black pepper, onion, and lemon juice. Blend until smooth.

2. Toss pesto thoroughly with hot spaghetti. Place on a serving platter and sprinkle with remaining 1 tablespoon Parmesan cheese. Serve immediately.

MAKE-AHEAD MEAL DIRECTIONS

To Freeze: Complete step 1 of the recipe. (Note: Do not continue to step 2.) Place spinach mixture in a 1-pint freezer bag. Seal bag tightly, allowing no excess air to remain, and freeze. This can be kept frozen for up to 1 month.

To Prepare for Serving: Let mixture thaw completely. Place in a medium saucepan and, stirring occasionally, heat thoroughly over medium heat. *Do not boil.* Toss with spaghetti and serve as directed in step 2 of the recipe.

CHILI-CHEESE TART

Serves 4   **Approximately 10.8 g fat, 127 mg sodium per serving**

Green-chili-and-cheese crustless tart served with baked tomatoes.

Low-calorie cooking spray
4 eggs
¼ cup evaporated skim milk
½ cup (2 ounces) shredded
   mozzarella cheese
½ cup (2 ounces) grated low-
   sodium, reduced-fat cheddar
   cheese
1 2-ounce can green chilis,
   undrained
Dash freshly ground black pepper
2 large tomatoes, halved
2 teaspoons Dijon mustard
1 slice reduced-calorie bread,
   toasted and grated
1 tablespoon chopped fresh
   parsley

1. Preheat oven to 350° F.
2. Coat a 9-inch pie pan with a low-calorie cooking spray. Add eggs and milk, and beat well. Stir in mozzarella and cheddar cheeses, green chilis, and black pepper.
3. Coat each tomato half with ½ teaspoon mustard. Top with bread crumbs and parsley. Place tomatoes on a foil-lined oven rack and bake with tart for 25–30 minutes.
4. Arrange tomatoes on a serving platter. Let tart stand 5 minutes before slicing. Slice in fourths and arrange on serving platter, alternately with tomato halves.

MAKE-AHEAD MEAL DIRECTIONS

To Freeze: Complete steps 1–2 of the recipe. (Note: Do not continue to step 3.) Bake tart for 25–30 minutes. Let cool completely, wrap tightly with freezer foil, and freeze. This can be kept frozen for up to 1 month.

To Prepare for Serving: Let tart thaw completely. Preheat oven to 350° F. Coat each tomato half with ½ teaspoon mustard. Top with bread crumbs and parsley. Place on a foil-lined oven rack and bake for 10 minutes. Place wrapped tart in oven and bake with tomatoes for 18–20 minutes. Serve as directed in step 4 of the recipe.

❦ ❦

SPINACH AND CHEESE–STUFFED PASTA SHELLS

Serves 4

Approximately 2.5 g fat, 481 mg sodium per serving

Low-calorie cooking spray
1 cup sliced fresh mushrooms
½ cup chopped yellow onion
¼ cup finely chopped green bell
  pepper
2 garlic cloves, minced
1 cup no-salt tomato sauce
1 cup chopped fresh tomato
½ cup water
2 tablespoons dry red wine
¾ teaspoon dried oregano leaves
¼ teaspoon dried basil leaves
¼ teaspoon fennel seed
1 teaspoon sugar
⅛ teaspoon freshly ground black
  pepper
1¼ cups low-fat (1 percent fat)
  cottage cheese
1 cup (½ 10-ounce package) frozen
  chopped spinach, thawed and
  squeezed dry
¼ cup chopped fresh parsley
Pinch ground nutmeg
2 egg whites
16 cooked jumbo pasta shells (no
  salt added during cooking)
¼ teaspoon salt (if desired)
1½ tablespoons Parmesan cheese

1. Preheat oven to 350° F.
2. Coat a 10-inch ovenproof nonstick skillet with a low-calorie cooking spray. Over high heat, sauté mushrooms, onion, green pepper, and garlic for 2–3 minutes or until tender but still crisp. Add tomato sauce, tomatoes, water, wine, oregano, basil, fennel, sugar, and black pepper. Reduce heat, cover tightly, and simmer for 25 minutes.
3. While sauce is simmering, place cottage cheese, spinach, 2 tablespoons parsley, nutmeg, and egg whites in a food processor or blender and blend thoroughly. Stuff each shell with approximately 2 tablespoons cheese mixture.
4. When sauce is done, stir in salt. Arrange stuffed shells on top of sauce in skillet. Cover and bake for 40–45 minutes, or until thoroughly heated. Top with Parmesan cheese and remaining 2 tablespoons parsley.

MAKE-AHEAD MEAL DIRECTIONS

To Freeze: Complete steps 2–3 of the recipe. (Note: Do not continue to step 4.) When sauce is done, stir in salt. Pour sauce into an 8-inch square foil pan. Arrange stuffed shells on top of sauce. Let cool completely, wrap tightly with freezer foil, and freeze. This can be kept frozen for up to 1 month.

To Prepare for Serving: Let shells and sauce thaw completely. Preheat oven to 350° F. Place wrapped container in oven and bake for 45–50 minutes, or until thoroughly heated. Top with Parmesan cheese and remaining 2 tablespoons parsley.

THREE-CHEESE ZITI

Serves 4

Approximately 9.3 g fat, 393 mg sodium per serving

2 egg whites
½ cup evaporated skim milk
¼ cup skim milk
1 teaspoon Dijon mustard
2 tablespoons minced yellow onion
Low-calorie cooking spray
3 cups cooked ziti or any tubular pasta (no salt added during cooking)
¼ teaspoon freshly ground black pepper
¼ cup plus 2 tablespoons (1½ ounces) grated Provolone cheese
¼ cup plus 2 tablespoons shredded mozzarella cheese
½ cup (2 ounces) grated reduced-fat Swiss cheese
2 tablespoons freshly grated Romano cheese
⅛ teaspoon salt

1. Preheat oven to 325° F.
2. In a mixing bowl, combine egg whites with evaporated milk, skim milk, mustard, and onion. Blend well.
3. Coat an 8-inch square baking dish with a low-calorie cooking spray. Place cooked pasta on bottom of dish and sprinkle with ⅛ teaspoon freshly ground pepper. Pour egg mixture over noodles. Top with provolone, mozzarella, and Swiss cheeses. Sprinkle with Romano, salt, and ⅛ teaspoon black pepper.
4. Bake uncovered for 25–30 minutes. Before serving, let stand 5–8 minutes to set.

Do Not Freeze

❧ ❧

CHEESY VEGETABLE-STUFFED POTATOES

Serves 4

Approximately 8.6 g fat, 412 mg sodium per serving

4 8-ounce baking potatoes
Low-calorie cooking spray
1 cup julienned zucchini
2 cups quartered fresh mushrooms
1 cup chopped yellow onion
1 cup chopped green bell pepper
1 cup chopped fresh tomatoes
½ teaspoon dried oregano leaves
¼ cup chopped fresh parsley
¼ teaspoon salt (if desired)
⅛ teaspoon freshly ground black
  pepper
¼ cup (1 ounce) grated reduced-fat
  cheddar cheese
⅓ cup (1½ ounces) crumbled blue
  cheese *or* ⅓ cup grated
  Parmesan cheese
⅓ cup (1½ ounces) shredded
  mozzarella cheese

1. Preheat oven to 350° F.
2. Wrap potatoes individually with aluminum foil. Bake for 1 hour.
3. While potatoes are baking, coat a 10-inch nonstick skillet with a low-calorie cooking spray. Over medium-high heat, sauté zucchini, mushrooms, onion, green pepper, tomatoes, oregano, parsley, salt, and black pepper for 5 minutes, stirring occasionally.
4. When potatoes are done, split and fluff gently with a fork, being careful not to tear skin. Spoon vegetable mixture on top of each potato. Top with three cheeses and bake 3–5 minutes longer, or until cheese melts.

MAKE-AHEAD MEAL DIRECTIONS

To Freeze: Complete step 3 of the recipe. (Note: Do not continue to step 4.) Let vegetable mixture cool completely. Place in a 1-quart freezer bag. Seal bag tightly, allowing no excess air to remain, and freeze. This can be kept frozen for up to 1 month.

To Prepare for Serving: Let mixture thaw completely. Bake potatoes as directed in steps 1–2 of the recipe. While potatoes are baking, place vegetable mixture in a medium saucepan. Cover and heat thoroughly over medium heat, stirring frequently. Complete step 4 of the recipe.

❋ ❋

ZUCCHINI LASAGNA

Serves 4

Approximately 6.7 g fat, 484 mg sodium per serving

Low-calorie cooking spray
2 cups thinly sliced zucchini
½ cup chopped yellow onion
½ cup chopped green bell pepper
4 *uncooked* lasagna noodles
1 16-ounce can chopped no-salt tomatoes, undrained
2 5.5-ounce cans no-salt-added V8 juice
2 tablespoons no-salt tomato paste
1¼ teaspoons sugar
¾ teaspoon dried oregano leaves
¼ teaspoon fennel seed
¼ teaspoon dried basil leaves
⅛ teaspoon salt (if desired)
2 garlic cloves, minced
1 cup low-fat cottage cheese
1 cup (¼ pound) shredded mozzarella cheese
¼ cup grated Parmesan cheese

1. Preheat oven to 350° F.
2. Coat a 10-inch nonstick skillet with a low-calorie cooking spray. Over medium-high heat, sauté zucchini, onion, and green pepper for 10–12 minutes, or until tender but still crisp, stirring frequently.
3. In a 6″ × 10″ baking dish coated with a low-calorie cooking spray, place 2 uncooked lasagna noodles. Top with sautéed vegetables.
4. In skillet, combine tomatoes with liquid, V8 juice, tomato paste, sugar, oregano, fennel, basil, salt, and garlic. Blend well and bring to a boil. Remove from heat and pour half of the tomato sauce over the vegetables. By teaspoonful, spoon ½ cup of the cottage cheese on top. Sprinkle with ½ cup mozzarella cheese, then 2 tablespoons Parmesan. On top of Parmesan cheese place 2 noodles, followed by remaining sauce. Bake uncovered for 55 minutes.
5. Top with remaining ½ cup mozzarella cheese. Bake 5–7 minutes longer, or until cheese melts. Remove from oven and sprinkle with remaining 2 tablespoons Parmesan cheese. Let stand 15 minutes before slicing and serving.

MAKE-AHEAD MEAL DIRECTIONS

To Freeze: Complete steps 1–4 of the recipe. (Note: Do not continue to step 5.) Let lasagna cool completely. Wrap tightly with freezer foil and freeze. This can be kept frozen for up to 1 month.

To Prepare for Serving: Let lasagna thaw completely. Preheat oven to 350° F. Place wrapped container in oven and bake for 45 minutes. Complete step 5 of the recipe.

TORTILLA PIZZA

Serves 4   **Approximately 7.8 g fat, 126 mg sodium per serving**

Large tortillas covered with fresh tomato, green chilis, Mexican seasonings, and two cheeses.

Low-calorie cooking spray
4 10-inch flour tortillas
1 cup fresh tomato, seeded and
  chopped
½ cup (1 4-ounce can) green chilis,
  drained
¼ cup finely chopped yellow onion
½ teaspoon chili powder
¼ teaspoon freshly ground black
  pepper
¼ cup (1 ounce) grated Monterey
  Jack cheese with jalapeño
  peppers
½ cup (2 ounces) low-sodium,
  reduced-fat sharp cheddar
  cheese

1. Preheat oven to 475° F.
2. Coat 2 cookie sheets with a low-calorie cooking spray. Place 2 tortillas on each cookie sheet. Top each tortilla with ¼ cup tomatoes, 2 tablespoons green chilis, and 1 tablespoon onion. Sprinkle lightly with the chili powder and black pepper. Top each with 1 tablespoon Monterey Jack cheese and 2 tablespoons cheddar cheese.
3. Bake for 5–7 minutes, or until cheese melts.

MAKE-AHEAD MEAL DIRECTIONS

To Freeze: Complete step 2 of the recipe. (Note: Do not continue to step 3.) Wrap each pizza separately with freezer foil and freeze. This can be kept frozen for up to 3 weeks.

To Prepare for Serving: Do not thaw. Preheat oven to 475° F. Unwrap pizzas and place on 2 cookie sheets. Bake for 10–12 minutes.

❧ ❧

CHEDDAR-ONION POTATO "SKINS" WITH SOUR CREAM

Serves 4   **Approximately 7.0 g fat, 391 mg sodium per serving**

Lightly browned potato slices covered with melted cheddar, topped with a dollop of sour cream, and sprinkled with green onion.

Low-calorie cooking spray
4 6-ounce potatoes, unpeeled and cut in ⅛-inch slices
¼ teaspoon salt (if desired)
¼ teaspoon freshly ground black pepper
1 cup (¼ pound) grated reduced-fat sharp cheddar cheese
½ cup light sour cream
½ cup chopped green onion
Paprika

1. Preheat broiler.
2. Coat 2 cookie sheets with a low-calorie cooking spray. Arrange potato slices in a single layer on cookie sheets. Spray low-calorie cooking spray lightly over all potato slices. Sprinkle with ⅛ teaspoon salt and ⅛ teaspoon black pepper.
3. Broil at least 5 inches from heat source for 4 minutes. Turn slices over. Sprinkle with remaining ⅛ teaspoon salt and ⅛ teaspoon pepper. Broil 2 minutes longer. Turn off oven.
4. Arrange potatoes over entire bottom of individual dinner plates in a single layer. Sprinkle grated cheese evenly over potatoes, ¼ cup per plate. Return to warm oven 2 minutes to melt cheese.
5. Top each serving with 2 tablespoons sour cream. Sprinkle 2 tablespoons green onion on each plate. Sprinkle with paprika and serve immediately.

Do Not Freeze

THE SOPHISTICATED SCRAMBLE

Serves 4   **Approximately 9.9 g fat, 473 mg sodium per serving**

Eggs scrambled with fresh asparagus and mushrooms, seasoned with blue cheese, and topped with bread crumbs.

¾ cup water
2 cups 2-inch-long pieces fresh
  asparagus
1 teaspoon olive oil
1 cup sliced fresh mushrooms
2 tablespoons minced yellow onion
3 eggs
5 egg whites
⅓ cup skim milk
1 tablespoon Dijon mustard
3 tablespoons (1½ ounces)
  crumbled blue cheese
⅛ teaspoon salt (if desired)
1 slice reduced-calorie bread,
  toasted and grated
1 tablespoon chopped fresh
  parsley
Freshly ground black pepper

1. Bring water to a boil in a 10-inch nonstick skillet. Add asparagus, reduce heat, cover tightly, and simmer for 3 minutes. Drain well, remove asparagus, and set aside. Wipe skillet dry with a paper towel.

2. Heat oil in the same skillet. Add mushrooms and onion, and sauté over medium-high heat about 3–4 minutes, or until tender. In a mixing bowl, combine eggs, egg whites, milk, and mustard. Reduce heat to medium and add egg mixture to skillet with vegetables. Cook 2 minutes, stirring occasionally. Gently stir in blue cheese, salt, and asparagus. Cook 1 minute. Top with bread crumbs, parsley, and black pepper.

Do Not Freeze

VEGGIE-STUFFED PITAS

Serves 4   **Approximately 9.8 g fat, 424 mg sodium per serving**

Pita bread filled with lettuce, tomato, avocado, alfalfa sprouts, and cucumbers, dressed with a touch of sour cream and cracked pepper.

4 pita rounds, halved
1 ripe medium avocado, peeled and diced
1 teaspoon fresh lemon juice
½ cup light sour cream
⅛ teaspoon salt (if desired)
2 tablespoons chopped green onion
½ cup alfalfa sprouts, packed
½ cup finely chopped yellow onion
½ cup sliced cucumber
¼ cup finely chopped green bell pepper
2 cups shredded lettuce
2 medium tomatoes, chopped
Freshly ground black pepper

1. Preheat oven to 350° F.
2. Wrap pita bread in aluminum foil. Warm in oven for 5 minutes. Remove and fill each half with diced avocado.
3. In a small mixing bowl, combine lemon juice, sour cream, salt, and green onion. Mix well and spoon about 1 tablespoon dressing inside each pita half. Fill pitas equally with alfalfa sprouts, onion, cucumber, green pepper, lettuce, and tomato. Top with black pepper and serve.

Variation: Omit avocado and use 2 cups chopped cooked turkey. This variation reduces the fat per serving to 4 grams and raises the sodium to 455 milligrams.

Do Not Freeze

PASTA SALAD WITH TOMATOES AND FETA

Serves 4

Approximately 9.5 g fat, 401 mg sodium per serving

¼ cup red wine vinegar
1½ tablespoons extra-virgin olive
   oil
1 tablespoon dried oregano leaves
1 teaspoon dried basil leaves
¼ teaspoon salt (if desired)
¼ teaspoon garlic powder
⅜ teaspoon black pepper
3 medium fresh tomatoes, peeled,
   seeded, and chopped
2 tablespoons finely chopped
   yellow onion
¼ cup finely chopped celery
4 cups cooked thin spaghetti,
   cooled (no salt added during
   cooking)
¼ cup chopped fresh parsley
2 tablespoons chopped capers
1 cup fresh tender spinach leaves
3 tablespoons (1½ ounces)
   crumbled feta cheese
Freshly cracked black pepper

1. In a 1-gallon freezer bag, combine vinegar, olive oil, oregano, basil, salt, garlic powder, and pepper. Mix thoroughly. Add tomatoes, onion, and celery. Mix well. Seal bag, releasing any excess air. Marinate in refrigerator overnight or at least 2 hours.

2. Place pasta, parsley, capers, and spinach in a salad bowl. Shake vegetable mixture in freezer bag. Add to pasta mixture and toss thoroughly. Sprinkle with crumbled feta cheese and freshly cracked black pepper. Serve immediately.

Variation: Omit capers and substitute 6 green olives, sliced thin.

MAKE-AHEAD MEAL DIRECTIONS

This salad has a more subtle character after freezing but is still delicious and flavorful.

To Freeze: Prepare dressing and coat vegetables as directed in step 1 of the recipe. Freeze instead of marinating. (Note: Do not continue to step 2.) This can be kept frozen for up to 2 weeks.

To Prepare for Serving: Let vegetable mixture thaw completely. Shake to blend seasonings and coat vegetables. Drain and discard dressing. Place pasta, parsley, capers, and spinach in a salad bowl. Add drained vegetables from freezer bag. Toss thoroughly and sprinkle with crumbled feta cheese and freshly cracked black pepper.

TACO SALAD SUPREME

Serves 4   Approximately 9.3 g fat, 402 mg sodium per serving

This south-of-the-border salad features its own edible container—a tostaco shell, which is a prepackaged fried tortilla shaped like a bowl. Tostaco shells can be found in the Mexican section of most supermarkets.

Low-calorie cooking spray
1 garlic clove, minced
¾ cup chopped yellow onion
¾ cup thinly sliced fresh
   mushrooms
¾ cup plus 3 tablespoons chopped
   green bell pepper
½ cup chopped celery
1 cup no-salt chopped canned
   tomatoes, undrained
1 cup canned kidney beans,
   undrained
⅓ cup dry red wine
2 teaspoons chili powder
1 teaspoon cumin
½ teaspoon dried oregano leaves
½ teaspoon sugar
⅛ teaspoon ground cloves
¼ teaspoon ground red pepper
¼ cup chopped fresh parsley
4 tostaco shells
2 cups shredded lettuce
1 medium tomato, chopped
¼ cup (1 ounce) drained canned
   mild green chilis
2 tablespoons chopped green
   onion
½ small avocado, diced
Freshly ground black pepper

1. Preheat oven to 350° F.
2. Coat a 10-inch nonstick skillet with a low-calorie cooking spray. Over medium-high heat, add garlic and sauté 1 minute. Add onion, mushrooms, ¾ cup green pepper, and celery. Cook until vegetables are tender but still crisp, about 5 minutes. Add canned tomatoes with liquid, kidney beans with liquid, wine, chili powder, cumin, oregano, sugar, cloves, red pepper, and 2 tablespoons parsley. Bring to a boil, reduce heat, and simmer uncovered for 20 minutes.
3. Heat tostaco shells in oven for 5 minutes. Cool and fill each with ¼ cup bean mixture. Place lettuce on top of hot bean mixture.
4. In a mixing bowl, combine tomato, 2 tablespoons parsley, chilis, green onion, and avocado. Mix well and spoon on top of lettuce. Sprinkle all with black pepper and serve immediately.

MAKE-AHEAD MEAL DIRECTIONS

To Freeze: Complete step 2 of the recipe. (Note: Do not continue to step 3.) Let bean mixture cool completely. Place in a 1-pint freezer bag. Seal bag tightly, allowing no excess air to remain, and freeze. This can be kept frozen for up to 1 month.

To Prepare for Serving: Let bean mixture thaw completely. Preheat oven to 350° F. Place mixture in a 10-inch ovenproof nonstick skillet. Cover and heat thoroughly over moderate heat, stirring occasionally. Complete steps 3–4 of the recipe.

THE CLASSIC MAIN SALAD

Serves 4

Approximately 6.8 g fat, 467 mg sodium per serving

¼ cup plus 2 teaspoons extra-virgin olive oil
3 tablespoons fresh lemon juice
¼ plus ⅛ teaspoon salt (if desired)
½ teaspoon dry mustard
¼ plus ⅛ teaspoon garlic powder
¼ teaspoon black pepper
5 cups shredded Romaine lettuce
5 cups shredded red-leaf lettuce
¼ small red onion, cut into rings
½ cup thinly sliced cucumber
1 cup sliced fresh mushrooms
16 cherry tomatoes
2 tablespoons grated Parmesan cheese
4 extra-thin slices Italian bread, crusts removed
1 tablespoon finely chopped fresh parsley

1. Preheat broiler.
2. In a small jar, combine ¼ cup olive oil, lemon juice, ¼ teaspoon salt (if desired), mustard, ¼ teaspoon garlic powder, and black pepper. Mix well and set aside (see Note).
3. In a large salad bowl, combine lettuces, onion, cucumber, mushrooms, and tomatoes. Set aside.
4. Brush bread slices with remaining 2 teaspoons olive oil and sprinkle with remaining ⅛ teaspoon garlic powder, ⅛ teaspoon salt, 1 tablespoon Parmesan cheese, and 1 tablespoon parsley. Place bread on a foil-lined oven rack about 5 inches from the heat source. Broil for 1 minute or until golden brown. Remove bread from oven and cut each piece into four points.
5. Pour salad dressing over salad and toss thoroughly. Top with remaining tablespoon Parmesan cheese. Serve with garlic toast.

Note: For a more robust flavor, make salad dressing a day ahead and refrigerate until used.

Do Not Freeze

SUMMER DAYS FRUIT SALAD

Serves 4   **Approximately 6.3 g fat, 240 mg sodium per serving**

Mounds of fresh fruit tossed with a shaved sweet citrus ice and served in a frozen glass bowl.

⅔ cup orange juice or any fruit juice
¼ cup fresh lime juice
3 tablespoons sugar
½ teaspoon orange zest
3 cups cubed watermelon
2 cups cubed honeydew melon
2 cups sliced strawberries
1 cup halved red grapes
2 cups thinly sliced peaches
1 cup unpeeled, thinly sliced apple
1 cup ½-inch pieces pineapple
½ cup diet ginger ale (if desired)
2 ounces "light" whipped cream cheese
12 slices white melba toast

1. In a mixing bowl, combine orange juice, lime juice, sugar, and orange zest. Blend until sugar dissolves. Freeze in a large glass bowl. (If there is not enough room in freezer, place in 1-gallon freezer bag, flat.)
2. After 1 hour, stir juice mixture. Continue freezing until almost firm, about 1 more hour. Stir again.
3. Combine fruit in a bowl. Shave citrus ice with edge of a spoon. If desired, pour ginger ale over fruit. Toss with shaved ice. Serve *immediately* with cream cheese and melba toast.

Variation: To make this even colder, place serving bowl containing fruit in freezer 15 minutes before serving.

MAKE-AHEAD MEAL DIRECTIONS

To Freeze: Complete steps 1–2 of the recipe, using a 1-gallon freezer bag rather than a glass bowl. (Note: Do not continue to step 3.) This can be kept frozen for up to 1 month.)

To Prepare for Serving: Let citrus ice thaw for 10 minutes. Break up into large chunks in bag and thaw 10 minutes longer. Shave with a spoon. Complete step 3 of the recipe.

❧ INDEX ❧